Praise for
LIVE LOVE LEAD

"History will record that God used Brian Houston to change the culture of the twenty-first-century Church worldwide like no other person. This great book is not only a life-changing story, but a valuable collector's document that you will treasure."

—Tommy Barnett, pastor, Phoenix First,
and founder, Los Angeles Dream Center

"I highly recommend this book to anyone who has taken a few detours or encountered some dead ends along the way. You will be encouraged and inspired."

—Jentezen Franklin, senior pastor, Free Chapel,
and author of the *New York Times* bestseller *Fasting*

"Pastor Houston's new book LIVE LOVE LEAD is a practical yet powerful message to all Christians, especially leaders."

—Casey Treat, senior pastor,
Christian Faith Center, Seattle

"If you're looking for safe, try sidewalks and swimming pools! If you want significance and impact, read this book! It's a winner, just like the author, Brian Houston."

—Rick Godwin, senior pastor and founder,
Summit Christian Center, San Antonio

"Brian's openness, frankness, and wisdom have helped me and inspired me to LIVE, LOVE, and LEAD, even when the going gets tough!"

—Charles Nieman, senior pastor,
Abundant Living Faith Center, El Paso

"No matter where we fall short, Pastor Brian reminds us that it's never too late to follow the greatest guide: Jesus."

—Christine Caine, speaker, author of
Undaunted, and founder of the A21 Campaign

"LIVE LOVE LEAD brings Brian Houston's powerful preaching and positive personality to the page and inspires us to experience the excitement that comes when we walk by faith, following Christ each step of the way."

—Chris Hodges, senior pastor, Church of the Highlands,
and author of *Fresh Air* and *Four Cups*

"Pastor Brian gives key insights to a full life both for you and for those you lead. His insights are profound yet practical."

—John Bevere, author and minister,
Messenger International

"Wow! What an extraordinary book, where my good friend Brian tells his story so candidly that we can't help but be inspired to greater heights."

—Phil Pringle, OAM, founder
and president, C3 Global

"I can't remember ever being this excited to recommend a book. Pastor Brian's life, love, and leadership have forever changed me, and I know that through this book, they will change you, too."

—Judah Smith, lead pastor, The City Church,
and author of the *New York Times*
bestseller *Jesus Is _____*

"Your heart will be stirred not only to dream big about your future, but to trust in the one who holds it all together."

—Nicky Gumbel, vicar, Holy Trinity Brompton

"LIVE LOVE LEAD grants us access to the heart and mind of one of the greatest visionaries of our time. It will change the way you see limitations as you reimagine the future God has planned for you."

—Steven Furtick, lead pastor, Elevation Church, and *New York Times* bestselling author

"There is no doubt you will be enlarged, empowered, and equipped by the wisdom and honesty contained within LIVE LOVE LEAD."

—Paul de Jong, senior pastor, LIFE

"Profoundly empowering in its wisdom and transparency, LIVE LOVE LEAD is an overdue glimpse into what I have been so blessed to witness my entire life. About time, Dad!!!"

—Joel Houston, Hillsong UNITED

"Brian lives by the principles found in this book, and I know they have the ability to transform your life and help you realize your potential to fully live, fully love, and fully lead."

—Robert Morris, founding senior pastor, Gateway Church, Dallas/Fort Worth, and bestselling author

"Brian Houston is the living example of how to navigate this journey called life…This book will be a blessing for so many."

—Carl Lentz, lead pastor, Hillsong New York City

LIVE
LOVE
LEAD

YOUR BEST IS YET TO COME!

BRIAN
HOUSTON

FaithWords

New York   Boston   Nashville

Cover art direction: Jay Argaet / Joel Houston
Cover art designer: Nathan Cahyadi
Cover photographer: Andrew Maccoll
Cover copyright © 2015 by Hachette Book Group, Inc.

FaithWords
Hachette Book Group
1290 Avenue of the Americas, New York, NY 10104
faithwords.com
twitter.com/faithwords

Originally published in hardcover and ebook by FaithWords in September 2015.
First Trade Paperback Edition: September 2016

FaithWords is a division of Hachette Book Group, Inc. The FaithWords name and logo are
trademarks of Hachette Book Group, Inc.

The publisher is not responsible for websites (or their content) that are not owned by the publisher.

The Hachette Speakers Bureau provides a wide range of authors for speaking events. To find
out more, go to www.hachettespeakersbureau.com or call (866) 376-6591.

Unless otherwise noted, all Scripture quotations are taken from the New King James Version of
the Bible. Copyright © 1982 by Thomas Nelson, Inc. Used by permission. All rights reserved.

Scripture quotations marked MSG are taken from THE MESSAGE. Copyright © by Eugene
H. Peterson 1993, 1994, 1995, 1996, 2000, 2001, 2002. Used by permission of NavPress
Publishing Group.

Scriptures noted NASB are taken from the New American Standard Bible®, Copyright © 1960,
1962, 1963, 1968, 1972, 1975, 1977, 1995 by The Lockman Foundation. Used by permission.

Scriptures noted NIV are taken from the HOLY BIBLE: NEW INTERNATIONAL
VERSION®. Copyright © 1973, 1978, 1984 by International Bible Society. Used by
permission of Zondervan Publishing House. All rights reserved.

Scriptures noted NLT are from the *Holy Bible*, New Living Translation, copyright © 1996. Used
by permission of Tyndale House Publishers, Inc., Wheaton, Illinois 60189. All rights reserved.

Scriptures noted KJV are taken from the King James Version of the Bible.

Hillsong Music credits are located on page 256.

Library of Congress Cataloging-in-Publication Data
Houston, Brian.
   Live love lead : your best is yet to come / Brian Houston. — First [edition].
      pages cm
   ISBN 978-1-4555-3344-2 (hardcover) — ISBN 978-1-4789-6301-1 (audio playaway) —
ISBN 978-1-4789-5956-4 (audio cd) — ISBN 978-1-4789-5957-1 (audio download) —
ISBN 978-1-4555-3343-5 (ebook)   1. Christian life.   I. Title.
   BV4501.3.H68184 2015
   248.4—dc23
                                                                              2015023094

ISBNs: 978-1-4555-3342-8 (trade pbk.), 978-1-4555-3343-5 (ebook)

*To the people of Hillsong Church, our family,
and the longtime friends who have stood
by Bobbie and me through every season of life,
love, and leadership—we are forever grateful.
May the Lord bless you and keep you and
make his face shine upon you...the best
is yet to come!*

Contents

INTRODUCTION
The Best Is Yet to Come   1

PART 1

A Big Life

CHAPTER ONE
Life in the Faith Lane   7

CHAPTER TWO
Comfortable in Your Own Skin   20

CHAPTER THREE
Confident in the Call   30

CHAPTER FOUR
Loving Unconditionally   42

CHAPTER FIVE
Pioneering   56

PART 2

A Difficult Path

CHAPTER SIX
The Worst Day of My Life   69

CHAPER SEVEN
Understanding the Process of Pain   79

CHAPTER EIGHT
Shame, No More   94

CHAPTER NINE
Lean on Me   104

CHAPTER TEN
The Original Pioneer   116

PART 3

A Narrow Gate

CHAPTER ELEVEN
No Other Name   133

CHAPTER TWELVE
Calling on the Name of Jesus   145

CHAPTER THIRTEEN
Discovering Narrow Is Never Tight   156

CHAPTER FOURTEEN
A Holy Calling   167

CHAPTER FIFTEEN
A Jesus Generation   178

PART 4

A Glorious Future

CHAPTER SIXTEEN
A Robust Kind of Faith   193

CHAPTER SEVENTEEN
My Lord, My God   206

CHAPTER EIGHTEEN
Hand and Heart   219

CHAPTER NINETEEN
Don't Stop   231

CHAPTER TWENTY
All Things New   245

The Best Is Yet to Come

The best is yet to come.

It's a declaration into the future, my firm belief that even the unknown can hold the greatest potential.

The Christian life is a life of unexpected adventure. It's as exotic as the Australian outback and as everyday as a cup of coffee. You can start wherever you are. It's never too late, even if you've taken a few detours and encountered some dead ends along the way. You only have to follow the greatest Guide who ever walked the path of life: Jesus.

Living fully, loving completely, leading boldly—these are the hallmarks of Jesus' time on earth. Whether you're taking baby steps or giant strides, walking on water or running on empty, wherever you are in your journey of faith, Jesus is the ultimate guide and companion.

Jesus lived fully present in each moment every day. He gave his attention, his heart, and his energy to those around him who needed him even as he advanced God's kingdom in the most dramatic way possible. He alone provides us with a model of a big, wide-open life fully lived.

We are all born with God-given potential to change the world around us. When you follow Christ, you can have confidence that despite the mysteries, setbacks, and disappointments that follow, the path Jesus leads us on is a path full of life—both in this age and the age to come.

Jesus' starting point was as humble and meager as it gets. He came from a small community, a tiny country; he was born in a dirty stable; and he was ostracized and criticized his entire life. His beginnings didn't dictate his future, and neither do yours. That's good news for a guy like me. Born in Auckland, New Zealand (one of the smallest countries in the world), to Salvation Army officers, my life has been as challenging as it has been deeply rewarding.

I've learned that it's not always easy to find your way, but Jesus gave us good directions: "Enter by the narrow gate; for wide is the gate and broad is the way that leads to destruction, and there are many who go in by it. Because narrow is the gate and difficult is the way which leads to life, and there are few who find it" (Matt. 7:13–14). This verse has been my road map for most of my life, and I pray that within these pages you will find gathered wisdom and encouragement, often acquired through trial and error, to inspire you along your own path of life and leadership.

We all desire to live a full life, an abundant life, a life over-flowing with purpose and passion. My journey is one of ministry and the Church. Yours may be vastly different. Whether you are in church leadership, business leadership, or—like most of us—involved in family and friendships that require our time and attention, these biblical truths remain consistent across circum-stance, challenge, geography, time, or even belief.

When we started Hillsong Church in a humble warehouse on the northwest outskirts of Sydney, I would look out my grimy office window and see undeveloped fields, weed-strewn paddocks where a few horses grazed, and an occasional truck searching for one of the handful of other warehouses nearby. A church full of people was a vision in my heart, but a far cry from the two hundred or so lovable misfits who regularly filled our pews.

From a young age, I knew I was called to build the church. Yet the personal journey of leading Hillsong Church into the healthy, thriving global community it is today has led me along a winding path of both criticism and accolade. My wife, Bobbie, and I have experienced both the mountain peaks and the valley depths in our endeavor to build the House of God, coupled with raising a family and maintaining a healthy marriage. Sometimes we have had to make hard decisions and take the road less traveled in order to maintain the purposes to which we felt called. Sure, we have lost our footing a time or two, but I have learned that in order to keep your eyes on Jesus through the ups and downs of life, you must keep your heart focused on the one thing he has purposed you to do. What is it that you feel called to do? And what is it that is getting in your way?

Sometimes our feet may fail as we try to walk through the narrow gate. Especially if we make the passage harder than it needs to be, tighter and more confining. When we allow our fears and insecurities to blind us momentarily, we're often tempted to make the gate narrower than God does. But don't be disheartened. God will always lift us up and sustain us if we're willing. He's promised never to leave us or abandon us on our journey— he's with us for the long haul.

As followers of Christ, we are called to follow in his footsteps, living a big life along a difficult path, journeying through the narrow gate toward a glorious future. God redeems us as his Spirit transforms us, making us more like Jesus each day. While rarely easy or predictable, this process brings more fulfillment to our lives than anything on earth.

In the chapters that follow, I want to explore what it means to live, love, and lead like Jesus along the twists and turns of this inspired road map from Matthew 7:13–14. First, we'll explore how to enjoy A Big Life before looking at ways to overcome the obstacles along A Difficult Path. Then we'll consider what it means to go through A Narrow Gate so we might enter into A Glorious Future. Living, loving, and leading like Jesus will enable you to experience more joy, power, purpose, and peace as you surrender every step of every day to the One who knows the beginning from the end.

It is my firm belief that following Jesus is the only journey in life worth taking. After seeing the way God changes hearts, meets impossible needs, heals incurable diseases, and restores people, I am convinced beyond a doubt that God didn't create us to live mediocre, settle-for-less lives. He sent his Son to die on the cross so that we could be forgiven and have eternal life, and not so we could sleepwalk through life as we wait for Heaven. The Word of God shows us how to navigate the inevitable twists and turns, and bumps and bruises we may encounter. God has a unique purpose and plan for you—your life, love, and leadership journey was crafted in Heaven long before the foundations of the earth.

Your spiritual adventure has already started—and the best is yet to come!

PART 1

A Big Life

CHAPTER ONE

Life in the Faith Lane

**You call me out upon the waters
The great unknown, where feet may fail.**
"Oceans," Hillsong Music, 2013

When following Jesus, be careful what you dream. Because you can rest assured that God will exceed the limits of your imagination if you're committed to advancing his kingdom. Living, loving, and leading like Christ will expand your life, stretch your heart, and deepen your faith. I know firsthand.

If you had met me at age twenty, you would not have nominated me in the "most likely to lead a global ministry" category. Although I was blessed with a loving family—my mum and dad and four siblings—and had grown up active in the church, I felt very awkward as a teenager. I was tall and uncoordinated; I was not a great student and was easily distracted. As I began to follow in my father's footsteps as a pastor and leader, I had to face the fear that so many people have of public speaking. The pressure of being a prominent preacher's son (which no one put on me but myself) caused me to be nervous and insecure, and I blinked incessantly whenever I had to speak in front of people. I didn't stutter, but my eyes did!

But I persevered, learning to relax and to rely on God, because I believed that leading was what God had called me to do. Deep down, I knew I was alive for a purpose bigger than I was, something more important than I could even understand or imagine as a young boy. I was determined that my frequent blinking and self-imposed anxiety would not prevent me from doing what I knew God wanted me to do. At an early age I awakened to the knowledge that God wanted me to serve him in ways that would make a positive difference in people's lives. So gradually, as my faith grew I began to experience his unfolding revelation of what he put me on this earth to do—lead, serve, and equip the local church.

Fortunately, I was blessed to be given a partner in living, loving, and leading—my amazing wife, Bobbie. Who knew that during a summer church convention, the beautiful young woman walking toward me on the beach, in a white swimsuit and carrying an ice cream, would care as much about ministry as I did? At the time, I just knew she was gorgeous! And, of course, she did bring me an ice cream. Several decades, three children, and a growing number of grandchildren later, our marriage continues to thrive, because we not only love each other but we love God first. Even when we first decided to get married all those years ago, Bobbie and I shared a dream to build the church, and be a part of a dynamic community of God's people growing, loving, and serving their family, friends, and everyone around them.

In fact, our dream of what a church could be arrived with quite a bang. During our engagement period, our constant conversation was about the future and our excitement to serve God together. At the time I was living in a house with a bunch of other single guys from our church. Bobbie and I had just finished getting a bite to eat when we began dreaming of the future.

Our excited discussion continued as I drove home and parked at the top of our neighbor Mrs. Wilson's very steep driveway. Bobbie and I often spoke about the price that we were willing to pay to serve God together—I remember vividly telling her that we may never own our own home or have financial security if we were to follow the call of God in our lives, and yet her constant enthusiasm made me love her even more. Caught up in the excitement of all that was ahead of us (including our wedding), we didn't even notice as the earth began to move beneath us. I was so invested in our conversation (and let's be honest here, a good-night kiss) that I had failed to engage the hand brake! I'm not sure Mrs. Wilson believed us when we tried to explain why we had crashed into her garage door at 2:00 a.m.!

Dream Crashers

The catalyst for that unfortunate crash continues to echo around the world in astonishing ways neither Bobbie nor I could've ever imagined that night in Mrs. Wilson's driveway. Today I'm about to hop on a plane to speak for the first time in our recently planted church in Copenhagen, Denmark. I'm smiling ear to ear as I recount the story I've just been told of an unchurched film executive in Los Angeles who was so greatly impacted at a recent event of Hillsong UNITED (an international worship band that emanated from Hillsong Church) at the iconic Hollywood Bowl that he began making plans so that "others can experience this"—the truth and emotion that worship had evoked in him. His is just one of so many stories.

The enormity of what is in front of us during each season of life could be daunting, and yet it is important not to lose perspective—we dreamed of these days! Days where influential people would sit up and take notice of the Living God and the impact of his Church on the globe.

My response to the way God continues to pour his favor on Hillsong Church and has used us to advance his kingdom mixes sheer joy with utter disbelief. Simply put, I'm astounded! Seeing Hillsong reach millions of lives around the world is more than two young kids in an old Nissan could have dreamed—it's witnessing God's power in action. It's seeing the small kingdom seeds we've been entrusted to plant over the past thirty years come to fruition. Living our lives sold out to God's kingdom cause has been the greatest adventure, and we continue to be excited about what he is going to do next!

In Australia we talk about cutting down the "tall poppy"—obviously referring to a flower that stands taller than all the others. It is an expression reserved for people who are doing more than most, or achieving unprecedented success. Often politicians, artists, entertainers, and businesspeople are scrutinized, and while this critical tendency can be used unfairly to take someone down a notch, it also reminds us not to think too highly of ourselves or assume all the credit. So let me be the first to cut down my own poppy, because I would never presume to take credit for any of the unbelievable and astounding endeavors that God continues to do through Hillsong. We're simply willing to serve, and we're blessed to be used along with so many others around the world who are building the Church and taking the good news of the gospel forward.

If I ever need to lower my own poppy a bit, I only have to remember how we started. You would understand if you could see the tiny apartment where Bobbie and I lived when we first moved to Sydney to serve in the church my parents had started there. If you could see me washing shopwindows for two dollars each (five for the really big ones) to make ends meet, if you could see Bobbie getting up early to help set up chairs for our service or painting clouds on the wall in the drab children's ministry area, then you would begin to grasp what God has done. If you could see me sitting on the piano stool with our green but gifted worship pastor, encouraging him to write church songs and lead people in worship. If you could see the little school hall where we first held services before we moved to a vacant warehouse surrounded by fields on the northwest outskirts of Sydney, then you would marvel just as we do.

Faith Outside the Lines

Life today is so different than it was when and where we started. In 1993, Hillsong Church was just ten years old. I sat down with a blank piece of paper in our office in Castle Hill. Looking out the window to forlorn shops across the road, I penned these words at the top of my journal: "The Church That I See." It was a bold declaration of the future, a fleece before God and the cry of my heart—a vision of the church I desperately longed to pastor. The statement spoke of international ministries, of influential music, and both convention centers and altars alike filled with people. I dreamed of television ministries not yet birthed and a college that seemed impossibly possible. It was a faith goal, and when I shared it with our church one Sunday morning I knew I had just stepped out of the boat.

Years later, we are living in the days dreamed about. The faith we had then wasn't even big enough for the depth of expansion and plans God had for our future. And what God has shown me again and again is that regardless of the level of success or expansive vision that we have, it all comes back to people. His heart is all about people. So as a result, I honestly see this as being about so much more than just numbers. Whether it involves membership, church budgets, weekend attendance, or music sales, I endeavor to look beyond numbers and see transformed lives. Too many people try to reduce faith and miracles into quantities, and I don't like trying to evaluate what God is doing by numbers alone. Faith can't be measured in square feet, dollars, and attendance figures. In fact, we remind ourselves regularly that Hillsong Church isn't about the crowd—it's actually all about the *one*. Like the one cabdriver in Guatemala who, with tears in his eyes, told us about the impact of Hillsong music on his broken family. Or the woman in Uganda who discovered we were from Australia and said, "There are only two things I know about Australia: kangaroos and Hillsong." Or the people we meet in the strangest places—from the remote beaches of Africa to the bathroom queues of the world's largest airports—who express their gratitude for the ministry of Hillsong and the impact that God has had on their lives through an encounter with one person, one song, or one message.

It is my belief that most of the evidence of what God is doing goes largely unnoticed and unrecorded. The family reunited after a parent discovers the love of Jesus and completes parole. The divorced person feeling accepted and loved just as she is. The secret addict finding the courage to share his struggle within a community of encouraging believers. The hungry child fed. The lonely widow comforted. The orphan parented. The estranged reconciled. The lost found. Seeing the way God raises the poor from the dust and lifts the needy, seats them on the level of princes, heals the broken, and calls the sinners righteous leaves me with no doubt that following Jesus is the only way to live.

Living in the faith lane isn't a paint-by-numbers picture. It colors outside the lines and sees with different eyes than the world does—eternal eyes with eternal perspective. Your Heavenly Father didn't create you to live a life of mediocrity.

He created you to live life in the faith lane.

Walking on Water

Living in the faith lane is not necessarily life in the fast lane. Instead of driving, maybe living in the faith lane is more like swimming. I've spent a great deal of my life near the water on the great beaches of Australia, swimming or simply enjoying a coffee at a beachside café. This sunburned country is the biggest island in the world, which means we have more coastline than anywhere else. My native New Zealand is composed of islands as well, and as a boy, there was nothing I loved more than being at the beach, floating in the cool water, finding relief from the summer heat.

But living in the faith lane is much more than just floating along, letting life's current carry you wherever it wants. Living in the faith lane is about taking control of your future while still depending on Jesus for every step you take—even when that means walking on water. That certainly seems to be the example beautifully depicted in the Hillsong UNITED song, "Oceans," and that we see from Peter's encounter with Christ one stormy night:

> Shortly before dawn Jesus went out to them, walking on the lake. When the disciples saw him walking on the lake, they were terrified.

"It's a ghost," they said, and cried out in fear.

But Jesus immediately said to them: "Take courage! It is I. Don't be afraid."

"Lord, if it's you," Peter replied, "tell me to come to you on the water."

"Come," he said.

Then Peter got down out of the boat, walked on the water, and came toward Jesus. But when he saw the wind, he was afraid and, beginning to sink, cried out, "Lord, save me!"

Immediately Jesus reached out his hand and caught him. "You of little faith," he said, "why did you doubt?"

And when they climbed into the boat, the wind died down. Then those who were in the boat worshiped him, saying, "Truly you are the Son of God." (Matthew 14:25–33 NIV)

A scrappy fisherman by trade, Peter can't believe his eyes when he and his fellow disciples look up and see someone treading the choppy waters toward them. It *has* to be a ghost—no other explanation. As if the brewing storm isn't enough. They are really terrified now.

Then they hear his voice.

"Take heart! Everything is okay! It's only me!" Their Master's voice echoes like thunder. "Could it be...?" the disciples ask themselves.

But Peter wants proof. "If it's really you, Lord," he shouts into the howling wind, "then tell me to come to you on the water!"

"Come!" Christ yells back without a moment's hesitation.

And then it happens. Peter gets out of the boat and takes a step. Locking eyes with his Master, the fisherman tries not to think about what he's actually doing and just lets his legs do something they've done countless times. One step, then another, and another.

He's walking on water.

But then Peter notices the wind picking up again and he panics. Maybe he starts thinking, "I'm walking on water! Wait a minute—that's impossible! Can't be done!" And then he begins to sink like a rock.

Row Your Boat

I know that sinking feeling.

One summer when I was nine or ten, my family was on holiday at a lakeside cottage next to one of the South Island's famous "bottomless" lakes. While our parents talked and relaxed with friends, my older brother and I noticed a small rowboat at the cottage next to ours and couldn't resist "borrowing" it. Now this lake was deep, and I've since learned it was notorious for sudden weather changes and currents. We had just gotten to the other side when things began to look ominous and only halfway back when the storm clouds came rolling in.

As the wind continued to pick up and the current got stronger, we began rowing harder—though home never seemed to get any closer. Our arms began to grow tired just as the unthinkable happened: I lost my oar.

"What do we do now?" I yelled out to my brother.

"Go get it!" he shouted back above the sharp whistle of the wind.

He was two years older than me, and my options were few—so I jumped into the water.

Big mistake.

Reaching the oar was relatively simple. But with the current pushing me away from the boat and an oar in one hand, my arms were tired from rowing, and the stinging rain burned cold on my face. I began to gasp for breath.

Then I saw my brother swimming toward me. He was as crazy as I was! At least he was willing to come after me, feeling responsible—or guilty—for telling me to go into the water. As he swam closer and closer, I wondered how he was going to be able to save us both. Wouldn't the current now pull us both under?

But big brother had a trick up his sleeve—literally. He had tied a rope from the boat to his arm. So he grabbed me and we began pulling the rope in, dragging the boat closer and closer until we could pull ourselves back into it.

By the time we made it back to shore to face our parents' punishment, the storm had cleared, and I had a newfound respect for what Peter and the other disciples must've faced out on the water that night.

I couldn't imagine trying to walk on the ever-changing surface of it. Impossible enough if the lake's surface was calm. But in a storm? *Beyond* impossible.

Unless you have faith. The kind that Peter had for those moments as he simply obeyed the Lord's command. The kind that he had before he started thinking about why he could not do what he was doing. The kind you have when you're living in the faith lane.

What is it that's ahead of you right now that feels impossible? What is the "middle of the storm, walk on water" task in front of you that feels immediately daunting and impossibly fearful? At some point, we all need faith to step out of the boat.

Step into the Great Unknown

So often we fail because we get stuck in our heads, tangled in our thoughts, mired in speculation and probability, grasping to make life work any way we can. We want to walk on water. But we insist on trying to do it under our own power. If we put our trust in something else—technology to control the weather, money for a bigger boat, or a life vest "just in case"—then maybe we can figure it out. But we can't! The moment we think we can is when we take our eyes off Jesus—and that's when we begin to sink!

Life is a journey, a winding path filled with many unknowns. It's only possible to navigate because of God's power and grace.

Maybe you will relate to this story: It was in late 2012 and Taya Smith, one of our talented young worship leaders and a member of Hillsong UNITED, was simply just another face in the crowd. Her singing ability went largely unnoticed in our church arena, yet she faithfully served behind the scenes in our youth ministry.

Taya was working in retail and was forced because of holiday hours to take some time off, during which she had planned to visit with her family in rural New South Wales. But she had waited too long to buy a plane ticket, and now the flights were too expensive. So she was stuck in Sydney with one week's holiday—the same week that our church was recording the album *Glorious Ruins*. She went into church that Sunday night and was told to "be ready to hop up" at the end of the recording if there was time and join the rest of our youth band Young and Free. That night she sang her heart out, and my son, Joel Houston, took notice of it.

That following Tuesday morning, Taya woke up with a message on her phone from Mike Chislett, Hillsong UNITED's producer, asking if she would come down to the studio to do some backing vocals for the new UNITED project. Taya doesn't have her driver's license, so for two days in a row she caught multiple buses and trains from her home in the south of Sydney, and then she rode her skateboard from the train station to the UNITED studio in North Rocks—about one and a half hours each way. It was during those two days that Joel gave her a new song to learn, and Taya recorded "Oceans."

The story goes that once she finished the first take, she turned to the boys and nervously said, "I can do better." Taken aback, they replied, "That was pretty good, though." (If you have ever heard Taya sing, you can imagine how much heart and passion she puts into absolutely everything she does.)

I love how Taya recounts riding the bus home that night and recalling the prayer that she had prayed only two weeks before: asking God to either open or shut the door on an opportunity to sing professionally—and feeling the Lord's prompting to lay that dream aside to step into the great unknown. The rest is history.

Taya's story is like so many. A young girl stepped out, God got in the way of her plans, she chose service over convenience, and her life today is a testimony to her faith and the faithfulness of God when we trust him with the unknown details of our lives.

If you want to live, love, and lead like Jesus, then there's no other place to live but in the faith lane. To discover his plan for your life, you will need to step into the great unknown, risking everything you have. If you get out of the boat and follow the sound of his voice, you will take steps you never thought possible.

You will begin a mystery tour, an excursion to his unspecified destinations. You will come alive with the possibility of relying on God to do what seems impossible. You will find yourself challenged, stretched, and tried and tested. You may even walk on water.

This is life in the faith lane!

CHAPTER TWO

Comfortable in Your Own Skin

Here I am down on my knees again
Surrendering all.

"I Surrender," Hillsong Music, 2012

I love mornings at home in Sydney when I have ample time to get up and about. When I wake up on those days, it's usually quite early, so I rummage around in the dark in a vain attempt not to wake Bobbie. I'm bleary-eyed and still half-asleep, but my routine is so familiar I don't have to think about it. I find my Nike T-shirt, some basketball shorts, my running shoes, and my favorite old cap (so I don't have to do my hair). While the other items might get commandeered by my wife for the laundry bin, it's the same cap every day.

After I'm dressed I slip out the door to get that first morning coffee at the Tuck Shop just a few blocks away. The air still feels cool before the sun burns across the Australian sky. Along with a handful of other early birds, I reach the coffee shop and sit at a small corner table, sip my coffee, and meditate on the day ahead.

These slow, stay-at-home preparation mornings are my favorite, because I can stay in my favorite, most comfortable clothes. It's funny because if I run into someone I know, they'll ask, "Have you been exercising?" or "Did you have a good run?" Then I have to confess, "No, this was just the easiest thing to put on!" But sometimes my clothes do motivate me to head out on a (very slow) jog around the neighborhood—where there's life, there's hope—before I hit the shower and get on with the rigors of the day. Mostly they just make me feel good—I'd live in those clothes if I could!

Fits Like a Glove

You probably have your own special items that have become your favorites over the years: a pair of old jeans, a leather jacket, a concert T-shirt, or a first-date dress. Such pieces not only fit like a glove but they're also very comfortable. You feel good wearing them.

Don't you wish your life felt as comfortable as your favorite clothes? That you felt just as comfortable in your own skin as you do in your favorite pair of jeans? That your life expressed the alignment of who you are with who God made you to be?

I'm convinced that we all long for this kind of life. We see it displayed sometimes by individuals who discover their calling, embrace it fully, and then excel at levels off the chart. People living in this gracious rhythm that combines their passion, talents, abilities, and opportunities seem to stand out. We admire their achievements and are inspired by their contributions to others around them, the way they love living life and do it with seemingly effortless grace.

Although you can find them in every field and arena, I often notice this special quality in my favorite athletes. The very best sportspeople—whether in America's NBA or NFL, or Australia's sport of choice—just recognize their strengths and play into them. As a dedicated fan in a sports-loving country like Australia, I'm enthralled to see a gifted athlete at the top of his or her game. Watching them drive and score, lunge for a crucial tackle, or sweetly bat a ball into the outfield reveals a rhythm and poise to their movements, an intuitive gift that's been sharpened by both strategy and improvisation.

For you it might be watching your favorite actor or singer perform, seeing a gifted teacher in the classroom, a skilled artisan carving a sculpture, or someone at home in the pulpit teaching with an ease that connects naturally with the hearts of people. You can see the same kind of performance in virtually anyone who excels at a level that combines their natural abilities, their deep-seated passion, their training, and their wisdom gleaned from countless hours of experience.

In his book *Outliers*, Malcolm Gladwell asserts that it takes ten thousand hours of practice, performance, drills, and more practice before someone transforms into one of those phenomenal people who becomes an icon in their field. Maybe you haven't put in your ten thousand hours yet in one particular endeavor—or even discovered what your true calling is—but you likely have spent that much time being a student of yourself. You know you long for more purpose and a deeper satisfaction in your life.

You long for the big, wide-open, spacious kind of life Jesus came to bring.

Overwhelmed

Recently, Bobbie and I were driving along in the car, an hour away from our destination. We chatted about various matters, our kids and grandkids, people at church, before lapsing into that comfortable silence you enjoy with someone you've loved for a long time. Then just out of the silence, Bobbie turned to me suddenly and said, "Do you ever feel overwhelmed?"

I had no doubt she was thinking about the Colour Conference for Women that she leads each year. Burdened by God's Spirit to create a conference that focused on how much he loves and values all women, Bobbie has seen the Colour Conference grow into an international event drawing thousands and thousands of women from around the world. Knowing this year's event was quickly approaching, along with the many other people and concerns she was juggling in her heart, I knew exactly where her question was coming from. As soon as she asked the question, without hesitating I answered, "All the time."

To be honest, we've never known a time when we haven't felt out of our depth. When we were young, we didn't have the resources or the experience to feel confident in what we were doing, so we had to rely on God each and every day. Then when we got a few years under our belt, both our family and our church family began growing and developing, and this always kept us on our toes, improvising under God's grace, looking to him for guidance, provision, and protection.

Then, as he has entrusted more responsibilities and resources to us, we feel even more overwhelmed. We could never do what we do by ourselves, not even with the thousands of amazingly gifted people who join us in advancing the kingdom. But God keeps calling us, and we keep answering and acting on the prompting of his Spirit. And he has been more than faithful in providing all we've needed and more. But it's never been through our own power, talents, abilities, or influence.

Perhaps you, too, can feel overwhelmed. Maybe you feel trapped, caught in a cycle of tasks and bills and deadlines and not enough hours in the day. Life is certainly full of overwhelming moments, especially for those of us who want to do something worthwhile with our lives, to live with a sense of purpose. So often people look for answers in busying themselves with pursuits that end up draining them of energy and leave them fiercely lacking in motivation...and yet there is a better way to live.

The Bible has so much to say about living in grace—knowing, walking, and living in the undeserved favor of a kind and merciful God. The Bible is full of characters who felt out of their depth at times, inadequate for the task placed in front of them. Men and women overwhelmed by the purpose set before them and the call God placed upon their lives. People like Mephibosheth, who was a foreigner in a king's house. Moses, who was slow in speech. David, who was just a mere shepherd boy. Even a prostitute named Rahab, who was asked to betray her own people in order to save her family and trust a God she barely knew.

Time and time again, no matter who it is, they were all overwhelmed. And yet God gave them sufficient grace to fulfill their unique purpose and calling. I have to trust he does the same for you and me today. When the apostle Paul asked God to remove his "thorn in the flesh," a recurrent struggle, God answered him by saying, "My grace is sufficient for you, for My strength is made perfect in weakness," which in turn prompted Paul to write, "Therefore most gladly I will rather boast in my infirmities, that the power of Christ may rest upon me" (2 Cor. 12:9).

Your Own Sphere of Grace

While each person's story in the Bible gives us clues about how to live in the comfort of our own grace, the apostle Paul speaks of it directly. In almost every letter he wrote, whether to the Romans, the Ephesians, the Colossians, or whoever, he begins by introducing himself within the context of grace. In each case he exudes a clear confidence and natural strength, a real ease with himself. He has lost his limitations and instead focuses on what he's been called to do, trusting in God's power to accomplish it.

Notice how he begins his letter to the Ephesians: "Paul, an apostle of Jesus Christ by the will of God, to the saints who are in Ephesus" (Eph. 1:1). It seems a natural way to begin a letter, I suppose, but if you stop and consider it, his confidence shines through. Paul basically says, "*Paul*—this is who I am. *An apostle*—this is what I do. *Of Jesus Christ*—this is who I do it for. *By the will of God*—this is my authority. *To the saints who are in Ephesus*—this is my audience." In one brief sentence, Paul has revealed his entire sphere of grace!

Paul clearly had a confidence in what he was about. He was comfortable with his calling despite the challenges, which were often many, comfortable in the way God had uniquely dispensed grace in his life. When forced to defend his ministry and God's authority for its basis, Paul provides the best definition of this unique measure of grace that we are each given. He wrote, "For we dare not class ourselves or compare ourselves with those who commend themselves. But they, measuring themselves by themselves, and comparing themselves among themselves, are not wise. We, however, will not boast beyond measure, but within the limits of the sphere which God appointed us—a sphere which especially includes you" (2 Cor. 10:12–13).

He makes it clear that it's unwise to compare or assess ourselves based on our own standards or those of others. We can only operate within the sphere of service God himself has assigned to us. Whenever you start living your life by comparison, you will always end up dissatisfied, envious, resentful, jealous, and bitter. The grass will always appear greener beyond your own fences. You can always find someone who appears to be doing better than you, succeeding more than you, enjoying life more than you, making more money than you.

But if you understand what Paul means and look at how he lived his life, then it's clear that his confidence, his comfort in his own skin, came from living within this sphere, this measure of grace, God had given him.

I remember clearly the first ever ministry trip that Bobbie and I took together to America. We were invited to speak at a conference on the West Coast, and Bobbie and I were feeling a bit unsure, because it was our first time ministering in the United States. We had heard some things about ministry in the United States, like "pastors' wives only wear skirts" and none of the other speakers there had a ponytail like I did. We arrived feeling a bit sensitive about our "Australian-isms," and I remember sitting and listening to the other conference speakers so eloquently teaching in their polished American accents and thinking to myself, "What am *I* doing here?!" Yet it was the words of one of our good friends in ministry that brought me back to reality. As I was getting up to speak, he patted me on the back and said, "Brian, just be yourself. Be Australian—that's why we love you!"

We can be so distracted by our own insecurities, trying to fit into the boxes of other people's expectations and putting pressure on ourselves to be someone different. To this day, while I am entirely comfortable and confident in who I am, there are still times when I can momentarily feel out of my depth. But, as Oscar Wilde reportedly said, "Be yourself. Everyone else is already taken."

By living out his own special measure of grace, Paul accomplished amazing things for the kingdom of God. He reached across most of the world known to exist in his time with the good news of the gospel. He wrote letters of truth given by God's Spirit to inform, to instruct, and to inspire generations of readers and believers. He faced danger and stared down death on many occasions, and he was calm and centered in the midst of storms, shipwrecks, hostile crowds, and prison riots.

Paul repeatedly makes it clear that he is not the one responsible for the grace-based life he was living—only his relationship with God through the power of Christ fueled his confidence and contentment.

Blessed for Success

When you live within the parameters of your own special grace, then life feels open and expansive. You stop comparing and start appreciating. The abundant life Jesus came to bring us frees us from the confines of culture, competition, and comparison. We can be generous, inclusive, and grace filled, enjoying the fulfillment of our purpose as we love others just as we are loved. When we live out of the free, unmerited favor of God, we discover his grace is all-encompassing and all-sufficient. Through the power of his grace, God can turn around the most devastating sin or failure in our lives. His grace provides an answer to every problem, a way through any obstacle, an enabling power to do what we cannot do in our own power.

When you're living the full, abundant, wide-open life for which you were designed, everything you do will be characterized by passion, purpose, perspective, and peace. You'll be excited to wake up each morning, eager to get out of bed and get on with the day that the Lord has made and set before you. Hard work and unexpected obstacles won't deter you or frustrate you for long, because you know you're doing what you were made to do, being your most authentic self, liberated by the grace of God.

Just as Paul personalized the grace he had been given, you must embrace the grace God has given you. When you live inside your own sphere of grace, when you lose the limitations of living up to anyone else's expectations, then you become comfortable with yourself and your life in a way that feels like putting on your favorite clothes.

God has dealt each one of us a measure of grace. That measure is *all* you need to fulfill the purpose of God in your life. It may sound a bit far-fetched or oversimplified, but each one of us is born with uniquely tailored gifts and latent abilities, individually matched to our own unique purpose in life. Discovering this fact and living in the power of it is what will release you into a large and expansive life—a life you perhaps could only ever dream of, that you thought was just for the lucky ones. The key to the future you hope for is found in being faithful with the measure God has given *you*.

This personal measure of God's grace gives you an authority and stability. It's not based on who you are, who others think you are, or your performance. Whether you're a stay-at-home mom, a business leader, an artist or a tradesman, or a little bit of all of these, if you are living out what God has graced you to do, then you have his backing and support, his resources and favor. You have passed through the portal of perhaps into the vast wilderness of wonder! Comfortable in your own skin—this is where God wants you to live your life.

CHAPTER THREE

Confident in the Call

I'm caught in the rhythms of grace, they overcome all of my ways
realigning each step every day to live for your glory.
"Rhythms of Grace," Hillsong Music, 2011

When our kids were young and still at home, we would take every chance we got to head up to our little shack on the beautiful banks of the Hawkesbury River. In addition to being perfectly picturesque, it was also the ideal spot for water sports and doing all the things that kids love to do. We would water-ski, wakeboard, and soak up the sun before enjoying lovely summer evenings on the patio: swatting flies, being pestered by mosquitoes, and filling the night air with friendly family banter.

We were always accompanied by our two faithful golden retrievers, Jack and Moses. They would run for hours along those swampy riverbanks chasing every boat on the water. All our neighbors knew our dogs and were (mostly) amused by them.

When they weren't in the water or barking after boats, the dogs pursued their other favorite pastime: searching for rabbits, snakes, lizards, and anything that moved at ground level.

I was always shocked by the change in old Jack's slow and nonchalant demeanor whenever he caught one of those huge Australian lizards. It was like a different spirit possessed him. With the speed of a young pup, he would catch the doomed lizard in his mouth and shake it so violently that its neck would break in an instant. So proud, Jack would then return his lifeless trophy to my feet, although it was not exactly something I wanted to see.

I guess I shouldn't have been so surprised. Born to be a retriever, Jack was simply doing what he was created to do. He was doing what came naturally to him, even though no one had told him how to do that.

What a sad day it was a few years later when we were up at the cabin and found old Jack floating in the river. He was a strong swimmer, so Bobbie and I wondered what had happened. Was he hit by a boat? Did he have a heart attack while trying to swim across? Did his longtime buddy Moses jump on his back in the deep waters and accidentally drown him? We will never know.

We buried him under one of the huge pine trees where he loved to lie for hours. He was such a beautiful, placid family dog, but I never forgot seeing him in action whenever he spotted a lizard. Whatever the circumstances were when he passed, I knew he had lived a full life doing what he was born to do.

Discovering Your Unique Grace

Unfortunately, many of us aren't as comfortable in our own skin as my old friend Jack clearly was. Many people live out their whole lives and never feel confident about who God intended them to be.

Gideon struggled with this reality. In fact, Gideon was a man we could all relate to. Has God ever asked you to do something that seemed impossible? Have you ever hidden from a task that was in front of you, made desperate excuses to get out of something that seemed unavoidable or for which you felt inadequate and ill equipped? Well, Gideon did. Just like the feelings we discussed in chapter 2, he was overwhelmed. Let me set the scene...

In Judges 6, we read that Gideon, a warrior and member of the army fighting against the Midianites, was hiding out in a winepress, cowering from the enemy when an angel of the Lord appeared to him and said, "The Lord is with you, Mighty man of Valor!"

Mighty man? Ha! What could the angel have possibly been thinking?! Surely he'd made a mistake, delivered the message to the wrong person. Gideon the coward, a mighty man? Of valor?

Mighty indicates superior power or strength. *Valor* speaks of boldness, bravery, and courage in the face of great danger. When you picture a "mighty man of valor," what comes to mind? Perhaps a tall, strong, and fearless soldier who makes women weak at the knees and warriors tremble. Yet the so-called mighty man of valor, who trembled before this awesome angelic messenger of God, was a cowardly, disheveled, defeated combatant, hiding what little he had from those he might have to share it with.

The moment the angel declared over Gideon what he could not see in himself, doubts and excuses rose up inside him. Gideon's immediate response to the angel in verse 13 was, "O my lord, if the Lord is with us, why then has all this happened to us? And where are all His miracles which our fathers told us about, saying, 'Did not the Lord bring us up from Egypt?' But now the Lord has abandoned us and given us into the hand of Midian" (NASB).

"Oh, if, why, where, but!" he pleaded in a single breath. Sound familiar?

You see, in Gideon's day the people of Israel weren't exactly experiencing the Promised Land that had been intended for them. Their repeated disobedience had led to their land being overrun with enemies—other tribes were destroying crops, taking what was not theirs, and terrorizing Gideon's people. It's little wonder Gideon brought his wheat to the winepress—a place where no one would be looking for him. Yet God found him.

Can't you just imagine the scene? Gideon was completely overwhelmed by his circumstances and feelings of inadequacy. Yet here was this otherworldly, angelic being speaking things that must have seemed ludicrous to his ears. Can you imagine how he must have felt? But something inside Gideon was stirred, something given up for dead...it was hope. He was living defeated by his surroundings and had given up all hope of the dream his forefathers had carried through the generations. Then the Lord turned to him and said, "Go in this might of yours, and you shall save Israel from the hand of the Midianites. Have I not sent you?" (Judg. 6:14).

Might? Strength? What could God see that he couldn't? Did you know that you, too, have strengths? Are you any quicker than Gideon to recognize your God-given strengths, or are you consistently overlooking the very things—talents, giftings, attributes—that God intends for you to use? Who does God say you are, and what has he called you to do? The key to living a life of purpose is being able to answer these questions. Much like Gideon, we need to discover a sense of purpose, an overcoming spirit, and faith in a God who calls us by name and who has gifted each of us with individual strengths.

Just like Paul in 2 Corinthians, we must be comfortable living within the gracious limits that Christ has uniquely bestowed upon us, in order to move forward with the future promise and purpose he has for our lives.

Grounded in Grace

I was five years old when I made the decision to accept Jesus as my Lord and Savior. As I shared earlier, as long as I can remember all I wanted to do was pastor a church and be a part of building God's kingdom. After I finished school, I went to Bible college and then began to serve in the local church wherever I could. Today, with more than forty years in ministry behind me, I am living my dream, and the passion to serve God burns stronger than ever. Yet I didn't always live in the knowledge or the understanding of my appointed sphere, understanding my strengths, embracing my weaknesses, and discovering my grace zone. There were many times when I seriously questioned myself and doubted whether in fact I could really do the things I longed to.

Looking at yourself against the size of your dream can quickly become more than anyone can handle. The truth is, the plans God has for you are *always* bigger than you are, and they are never going to be something you can pull off easily and in your own strength.

I can still remember being in Bible college at eighteen years old. There was a time when each student had to give a short devotional talk to the other students, maybe sixty or seventy people. The moment came for me to speak, and to this day I remember deliberately walking out the door, getting in my car, and driving in the opposite direction just so I wouldn't have to speak in front of them!

No one would have recognized or even guessed I had a leadership gifting on my life back in those early days. I didn't lead anything, didn't captain any teams, and certainly didn't stand up in front of any crowds. Today, I regularly stand before great crowds of people in large arenas, comfortably delivering a forty-minute message—but that was not always the case! It was when I became comfortable in myself, when I listened to what God had to say about me, that I was able to step into all that God had for me. It was then I discovered the unshakable truth that you will never come second by putting God first.

I remain convinced that God gives each of us our own grace, a special measure of blessings that line up exactly with his purposes for our lives. Sadly, it took longer than it should have for me to discover my grace zone—and yet I have realized that it is never too late to start living in that realm of reality. God always sees more in us than we can see in ourselves.

In the same way, you will never fulfill God's purpose for your life if you look outside yourself. If you focus on who other people are and what they're doing and all that they have, then you end up comparing yourself and coming up short. God has not called you to be anyone else's imitation. If you try to become who others want you to be—even when they're well-intentioned and love you—you will remain unsettled because you're not being the real you.

Knowing the measure of grace God has given you means you don't have to be somebody else. It's so liberating! You don't have to try to achieve any milestone or award to feel self-confident. You just have to be faithful with the measure of grace God has given you. *Faithfulness* means holding on to your purpose and trusting in God's goodness in the midst of all the peaks, celebrations, and mountaintops, as well as the trials, temptations, and tragedies that life throws at you. This is how you grow, grounded in grace.

Discovering Your Unique YOU

God isn't schizophrenic. He didn't create you one way, in order to use you another way. He knew exactly what he had in mind for your future when he formed you. His Word gives us a glimpse into the way God has designed each of us individually, to function in the measure or sphere with which he has uniquely appointed us:

> For I say, through the grace given to me, to everyone who is among you, not to think of himself more highly than he ought to think, but to think soberly, as God has dealt to each one a measure of faith. For as we have many members in one body, but all the members do not have the same function, so we, being many, are one body in Christ, and individually members of one another. Having then gifts differing according to the grace that is given to us, let us use them. (Romans 12:3–6)

What are your strengths? Can you identify the unique giftings that are on your life? Because they are there, whether you recognize them or not. I remember distinctly a conversation that occurred with a man who had sought counseling at our church. He was sitting in the office, downtrodden and with an overwhelming sense of hopelessness. After a series of misfortunes, his self-esteem was in the gutter, and he was certain that his life lacked purpose. He had created in his mind a mile-long list of the things he had failed in his lifetime, and the things he could not do.

Finally, the counselor said to him, "How about we make a list of the things you *can* do?" Reluctantly, and after much hesitation, he finally said, "Well, I know how to fix a car, I guess." After a few moments more, he shared that he was good at helping his mother and father and was quite competent around the house. He continued out loud as he recalled his ability to make people laugh and to cook and to work in the garden. Within half an hour, he had created a long list of things he *could* do, and his entire demeanor had changed. He left the office a different person that day, confident in the strengths he did have and the unique set of skills entrusted to him.

You see, it is easy to fill your mind with what you do not have and lose sight of what God can do with what you *do* have.

Some people are uniquely graced for business, others for ministry or for motherhood, and the list goes on! Perhaps you are graced with the gift of generosity or the gift of compassion—a heart that breaks for the hurting and the needy. What a beautiful gift to have! We're told, "As each one has received a gift, minister it to one another, as good stewards of the manifold grace of God" (1 Pet. 4:10). Here *manifold* literally means the "manyfold" or "many-layered," the "multidimensional" grace of God.

Whether you are graced with the gift of leadership, the gift of athletics, or the gift of creativity, we are called to be good stewards and faithful servants of what is in our hand. No one is exempt, and if you didn't play your part we would be missing out on the unique grace and the individual strengths that you bring to the here and now.

There is a beautiful satisfaction that comes from knowing that we are doing exactly what God made us to do and are being obedient to his calling on our lives. It is as we discover our strengths, and grow comfortable in the grace we have been given, that we will begin to see the promises of God for our wide-open, spacious future begin to take shape.

Rhythms of Grace

For many people, "Hillsong" has become synonymous with the style of worship music that has come out of our church in the past few decades. In fact, I often get asked to explain our strategy for making Hillsong Music a global brand—which only makes me laugh and say, "It's a mystery, not a formula!" It's not that we haven't been deliberate or thought strategically about our music and how we share it around the world. It's simply that we could never have orchestrated the kind of phenomenal success that continues to show no signs of slowing down. Only God. Only his grace.

You see, God has blessed every ministry in our church in amazing ways, but the cup of Hillsong Music certainly overflows with an abundance of his blessings. However, it wasn't by trying to be anyone else that we found this remarkable favor and undeserved blessing—it was by finding our grace zone, deciding to be comfortable with being different and leaning in to the "sound" that was in our House.

I had decided long before we ever planted a church that I wanted to build a community of worshippers that influenced other churches. I love music, but even as the profile of Hillsong Music began to grow, I always understood that it was only because of the favor of God that, through our music, we were able to draw people into the church, and then cause them to look beyond the music to the message of the gospel.

In the early '90s, Hillsong Music had already gained credibility across the nation of Australia, and as churches sang our songs, a number of influential people in the American music industry began to take notice. People began to meet with us, and every executive I sat across from had a clear picture in their mind of what they believed would and would not work in North America. The general feeling was that in a day when Christian artists were gaining fame, the worship music of a church "just wouldn't sell," that our style would appeal only to young people, and that we should consider adapting to a more mainstream Christian market. Yet we were committed to doing what God had called us to do and what we felt was a unique spirit and sound that was not only working in our House, but by all reports was being used as a great blessing to others. We were simply living and leading out of the grace God had given us and being faithful to the heart of worship in our people and our church.

Then in 1995, Integrity Music, based out of Mobile, Alabama, offered to distribute our music. But within one week of our scheduled recording, our nationally acclaimed worship leader abruptly and unexpectedly left, virtually overnight. As you can imagine, this was quite a disruption. Not wanting to delay or cancel the live worship night, we scrambled and asked a talented woman who had been a faithful part of our worship team behind the scenes, Darlene Zschech, if she would lead worship that night—something she had never done before that time. Darlene is an incredibly humble and gifted individual and deserves every success that has ever come her way; but at the time I think she would agree that she wasn't expecting to be in leadership and had to be prompted, encouraged, and even gently pushed into the spotlight.

Just when we thought we had our problem solved, I realized we had to explain the situation to the producers and get them to approve our newest worship leader. They liked Darlene and agreed she was certainly talented enough to lead the project. However, they were a little concerned about how the audience would handle the fact that she was a woman in a leadership role—something that had never occurred to us and yet was quite revolutionary at the time!

To their credit, they took a risk, the album was recorded, and the rest, as they say, is history. Darlene did the job very well. The album was titled *Shout to the Lord*, which was also the name of her phenomenal song that has become one of the most renowned and contemporary classics for Christians all over the globe.

We had no hidden agenda for global success or for trying to make a statement about women's role in ministry. We were simply remaining faithful to what God called us to do, worshipping him with our whole hearts, even as we confronted new challenges along the way.

People will always have opinions, most of them well-meaning, about decisions made in faith. Many people have been quick to tell us over the years what a "London church" or a "New York church" should look like, feel like, and sound like—sometimes even suggesting that Hillsong culture may not fit in with the attitudes and mind-sets of a particular place. However, season after season we have been diligent to follow the promptings of God when it comes to planting churches in influential cities. And whether in London, New York, Paris, Kiev, or Cape Town, as we have committed to staying true to who we are and what we are all about, we have watched as each new church has experienced remarkable growth and blessing. We continue to practice this same attitude today, choosing to see each new obstacle as an opportunity for God to help us grow in our grace zones as we praise him along the way.

There's nothing to compare to this kind of satisfaction and the kind of confidence and contentment that comes from being exactly where you're supposed to be, doing exactly what God created you to do.

Follow your heart, stay true to the gift that is on your life, go forth in the strength that you have, be comfortable in your grace zone, be confident in your call—and watch as God exceeds your every expectation and leads you into a wide-open and spacious life.

CHAPTER FOUR

Loving Unconditionally

Everyone needs compassion, love that's never failing
Let mercy fall on me.
Everyone needs forgiveness, the kindness of a Savior.
"Mighty to Save," Hillsong Music, 2006

Pops, have you seen my Barbie doll?"

"Pops, look at me, I'm dancing!"

"Poppa...you're on the TV!"

I've got four granddaughters, two grandsons, six in all. I'm "that guy" when it comes to my grandkids—you don't dare ask me a question about them without being bombarded by photos and forced to listen to stories of their latest achievements and basic, every-waking-moment adventures. It's not unfamiliar to me that my constant bragging about them morphs into watching people's attention slowly fade away after several minutes of unrequited boasting. Being their "Pops" is one of my greatest joys. I used to tease my kids that I wanted them to have enough grandchildren to form my own rugby team, but these days it's looking more likely that I might end up with a ballet troupe. Regardless of what they choose to do with their lives, whether they love sports or prefer dancing in my living room, I love my grandkids and I always will.

Three of them are old enough to be approaching school age and play together frequently, two sisters and one cousin. Any two of them seem to get along quite well, sharing silly stories and giggling, but when a third joins in, then things become a bit chaotic. The old adage "Two's company and three's a crowd" is actually quite true in my experience.

Two of them can usually play together contentedly enough. However, when a third joins in, there's often a shift in the balance of power. Someone is bound to be left out. One wants something another one has, who in turn wants something the third one holds.

Such is the way of the world. We can get a small group of like-minded people to agree with us, but bring in someone who's significantly different than we are and the dynamic changes. Scripture directly addresses this relational dynamic: "Again I say to you that if two of you agree on earth concerning anything that they ask, it will be done for them by My Father in Heaven. For where two or three are gathered together in My name, I am there in the midst of them" (Matt. 18:19–20).

It's interesting to me that this verse speaks of two agreeing, but three gathering. Obviously, the more people that gather, the more difficult agreement becomes. When there is a crowd, we may agree on some things but we are not going to agree on everything. When you begin factoring in each of our individual backgrounds, special interests, and personal agendas, it's amazing how much we can disagree on! I believe that our fellowship with one another cannot be based merely on agreement. It must be based on Jesus, and on the love that he so readily gives to each and every person who calls on his name.

Even theologically, so many of us don't agree. Most believers usually agree on the fundamentals of the faith—how we view God, Jesus, the Holy Spirit, the cross and resurrection, and so on—but there are many areas in which we agree to disagree. And that's okay.

There's a world full of people out there with whom I don't agree and many of them don't agree with what I'm all about. When it comes to ethics and morality, many unchurched people might disagree with where I stand. Often people who have points of disagreement can be very passionate about their views. It seems these days that any person in authority who is building something significant has a collection of naysayers and bloggers ready to cut down and criticize anything and everything that they disagree with. Yet I believe we have to find a way to love other people beyond our disagreements. Even when we don't know how we can love someone so different from us, if we rely on the love of God, then we will find a way.

Just a few years ago I was approached by a major news outlet in our nation with an opportunity to support our state rugby league team before the biggest match of the year, one they had lost many years in a row. The idea was that I was to do a photo shoot in our team's jersey alongside other religious leaders, next to a headline that urged sports fans to "Keep the Faith." It was a fun article and one I happily and playfully went along with, tossing a footie around with my new acquaintance, a local Muslim imam. Sadly, as Christians, we can be so much quicker to build walls than we are to build bridges. This is not about compromising your beliefs; it is simply about loving the very people whom Jesus gave his life for. Did he and I agree on the fundamentals of faith and religion? Of course not—we are poles apart! But do we both support the same football team and lightheartedly pray for a miracle victory? *Yes!* Jesus was the master of crossing divides. He crossed gender divides, cultural divides, moral divides, and doctrinal and political divides.

I have always been firm in the belief that Hillsong Church and our ministry was going to be built on the things that we are for, and not on what we are against. We are for Jesus. We are for love. We are for his grace and forgiveness, for the healing and wholeness and transformed lives that come with saying yes to a relationship with Christ. We are for seeing you rise up, loosen shackles and shame built up by condemnation, and enter into a life of fulfillment and purpose—the life you were created to live.

Love Where It's Least Expected

If you want to love the way Jesus loved, if you want your life to be characterized by love in a way that reflects the heart of God to everyone you meet, then I recommend paying attention to how you respond to people who make you uncomfortable. You know, the ones who are different from you in significant ways, the ones you don't like, don't understand, and don't enjoy. The people who hold different beliefs, practice different lifestyles, and hold distinctly different priorities from your own.

While there are many different dimensions to Christian love, I believe the ability to love unconditionally is the one that most characterizes the spacious, abundant life we have in Christ. And I suspect this willingness to love others unconditionally and its regular practice are what's significantly missing from many believers' lives. We say we want to love others just as God loves us, but too often we end up choosing comfort and convenience over compassion. This is not the example set by Christ and not the way we are called to love.

As painful as relationships can sometimes be, we are made in God's image as relational beings, created to belong, to serve, to worship, and to live in community. God often provides for us and loves us through the people in our lives even as we're called to be his hands and feet to those around us. Relationships are the lifeblood of the Church, the Body of Christ.

As a result of his unconditional love for all people, we often find God in the midst of places and situations where we least expect him. On the street corners and in alleyways. In the hospitals and prisons, orphanages and courtrooms. Everywhere you find people, there you will also find God.

Yet, we're continually tempted to play it safe. We don't mean to become insular and self-righteous, exclusive and judgmental, but if we don't focus on our relationship with God foremost, then we're prone to becoming proud. We want to love all people, but unless we're consistently experiencing the love of Christ in our lives every day, then we end up trying to do it on our own. And the love required to love people different from us will always be supernatural.

In fact, don't forget that even Paul the apostle began his career as an angry Jewish legalist devoted to persecuting these upstart radicals who followed Jesus. It was only after Paul encountered Christ so directly and dramatically on his journey to Damascus that he discovered the fullness of living in God's grace, free to be himself as his Father created him and free to love others. As Saul, he was controlling, closed-minded, and driven by his own ego, but as God's beloved apostle, Paul became accepting, openhearted, and driven by his love for this God who had first loved him.

What frames the tone of your life? How often do you stretch beyond your comfort zone to reach out to people whom you are in disagreement with? The ability to enjoy a big, spacious, openhearted life is directly proportional to your ability to love everyone, especially those who are different from you.

What are your expectations of God regarding how you are to love others? What would you do if God called you into a place you didn't like or a situation that you disregarded? Would you struggle and suffer with your own prejudices and biases in order to share God's abundant love and merciful grace to people whom you dislike? God loves us without conditions, though too often we place conditions on our love before extending it to others.

I can guarantee that pastors these days will be asked certain controversial questions in media interviews. And their answers to these questions are always going to divide people.

I believe the Bible is clear on many of these subjects, and I have no intention of ignoring the Word of God. However, Jesus kept his harshest words for the religious bullies he encountered— and reached out to sinners and publicans, all with a measure of love and grace, in order that they might be saved. An adulterous woman, a serial divorcee (now living with another man), a Samaritan woman, a small-time con man, and a tax collector that he called down from a tree were among those he loved and treated with grace. Jesus didn't come to condemn the world. If God wanted to condemn the world, he would have sent a condemner. But he wanted to save the world, so he sent us a Savior (see John 3:17).

That's why it is sad to reduce any issue down to a single sentence or a media sound bite. We cannot reduce people's whole lives into one sweeping, judgmental statement filled with condemnation. Jesus never did that, and we must look at these issues through gracious eyes—through Jesus' eyes. I believe that we are bound by the Word we live by, the world we live in, and the weight we live with.

The Word we live by is obviously the Word of God. I cannot and would not want to unwrite the Bible. Yet the world we live in is continuously changing. I don't believe it is our job as Christians to squeeze the Word of God into the mold of the world, but it is our job to love the world that Jesus died for and it is our commission to reach all people. And the weight we live with is a heavy one. Many churches, whether you choose to acknowledge it or not, have young people who are growing up in good Christian families and yet are struggling with confusing issues of identity. Tragically, when they have tried to bring their struggles to trusted confidences, like youth pastors and friends, they have instead been alienated and ostracized. Perhaps well-meaning parents, who simply haven't known what to do, have sown words of rejection into their children's most vulnerable moments. The consequences of this are that time and time again we have seen these young people—who were once grounded and planted in church—end up hating God and despising every form of organized religion.

I care about young lives. I care about their futures, and the answer isn't compromising the Scriptures, but it is also not about reducing people's lives into unloving statements. It's about seeing what God sees—and loving others with the same unconditional love we have been shown by our Savior, Jesus Christ. People from all walks of life are welcome at our church, and I pray that when people walk through the doors they all feel a sense of welcome home. For "whosoever will to the Lord may come."

That doesn't mean that people don't need to change. The Christian message is a message of transformation, and we are all sinners saved by grace. Yes—God wants us to change, and

God helps us to change, but like Billy Graham said, "It is the Holy Spirit's job to convict, God's job to judge, and my job to love." Our world is full of disagreement. But thank God that our loving acceptance of people doesn't have to be built on agreeing with them. Our loving acceptance of them is built on the cross.

The Great Co-Mission

You and I are not the only ones who struggle with loving people who are different than we are. Jesus' disciples certainly faced this challenge as well, as did most people in the early Church. So much of Jewish religious law and cultural customs were based on rigid boundaries between what was holy and what was impure, what was sacred and what was common, what was pure and what was unclean. Elaborate rituals were carried out in order for a person to cleanse himself, and make himself worthy to enter the temple and present an offering to the Lord before the priests.

The Israelites knew they were God's chosen people. They had seen God lead them, protect them, and set them apart from other tribes and other nations. They were used to thinking of themselves as the only people God loved and favored. Such was the world of Palestine during Christ's lifetime.

However, Jesus came for all people, not just the nation of Israel. This was one of the most radical aspects of his message, the good news that anyone could be forgiven of their sins and have a relationship with their Heavenly Father. And Christ made it clear how important it was to take this message beyond the city limits of Jerusalem and the borders of Israel. After his resurrection but before his ascension, Jesus told his followers, "All authority in heaven and on earth has been given to me. Therefore go and make disciples of all nations" (Matt. 28:18–19 NIV).

We call this message the Great Commission, the co-mission we have to tell others about the love of God and how he manifested it by sending his Son to die on a cross for our sins. This message is the heart of God for all of his people. It always has been and always will be. When we encounter the Lord's mercy, grace, and forgiveness, his love for us becomes abundantly clear. Consequently, we can't wait to share it with others.

I love that thought that we are on a co-mission with Christ. In this together. So why do we let disagreement so often frame our discussion? Just recently we gave our entire church wristbands with the words "Missio Dei" on them. The back of the bracelet was meant to have the translation on it—"Mission of God"—but when we received well over forty thousand bracelets from our manufacturer in China, the engraving said, "Missio Dei, Mission of COD"! You have to laugh at it now, but at the time it caused a bit of anxiety for our communications and events teams!

The bracelets were to serve as a daily reminder for our church that each day we wake up we are "on mission," co-heirs with Christ and missionaries to the world around us. And to complete our mission it is important that we deal with the very things that may be holding us back or standing in the way of our connection with others. Christopher J. H. Wright, the English theologian and author, wisely said: "The mission of God's people is far too big to be left only to missionaries."

Today, I encourage you to align yourself with God's mission, the Great Commission. Step up and recognize the opportunity among your everyday encounters to love people with an extraordinary, unconditional love.

Available to All

One of the greatest examples of unconditional love that crossed every kind of cultural and social divide is found in Acts 10. This may sound like a distant story, but to you and me it may be the most significant chapter in all of Acts—it is the very setting in which the Holy Spirit became available to you and me, spreading beyond the people of the Old Testament and becoming accessible to all humanity. It's the story of two men whose worlds were far apart. One is Cornelius, a young, handsome, and strong centurion in the Roman army. As a Roman gentile, and in terms of the Jewish religious law, he was an outsider to the message of Christ. He was considered unclean and common, a soldier required to kill, and yet the Bible tells us that Cornelius loved God.

And then there's Peter, a young Jewish man, bound by Jewish law, who also defied the expectations of others. An untrained, uneducated fisherman, Peter was known to be a disciple of Jesus Christ.

Everything about this story is shocking. These two are polar opposites and yet God gives them both separate dreams, preparing them for a meeting that changed history.

Peter is staying in the house of Simon the Tanner, which is a mystery unto itself. You see, being a tanner was considered an unclean profession. Tanners constantly worked with impurities and animal skins, mixing together the most uncouth of materials such as dog dung and dyes in order to treat the leather. Peter, a Jew, should never have been there. But through a supernatural dream given to Cornelius two of Cornelius' servants end up knocking on the door of Simon the Tanner's home. They shouldn't have been there, either, yet they were acting in obedience to their master. The servants were instructed to fetch Peter and persuade him to return with them to Cornelius—an invitation he should never have accepted.

After receiving Cornelius' invitation, Peter might have been uncomfortable; he might even have been a little afraid or uncertain. There were plenty of Jewish zealots and Roman soldiers searching for Christians to beat, arrest, or kill. But Peter went where God directed him and acknowledged the all-inclusive, unconditional love shown by Christ on the cross. "Then Peter opened his mouth and said: 'In truth I perceive that God shows no partiality. But in every nation whoever fears Him and works righteousness is accepted by Him. The word which God sent to the children of Israel, preaching peace through Jesus Christ—He is Lord of all—that word you know'" (Acts 10:34–37). We are all sinners saved by grace.

Peter and Cornelius crossed countless divides that day in accordance with the voice and leading of God. Two men worked against all protocol in obedience to God's voice in order to reach more people with the love of Christ.

I want to treat the people perceived to be outsiders with the same respect Peter showed Cornelius. And as soon as Peter walked into the room, Cornelius fell to the ground and started to worship him. Once again, Peter was in awe! He immediately lifted the Roman soldier to his feet and said something like "Get up, man! I'm no better than you. Stand up and look me in the eye because I'm a man just like you" (see Acts 10:26).

Peter went on to explain that yes, usually Jewish people did not mingle with foreigners and those outside the nation of Israel; however, God showed Peter that he was to accept outsiders and share the gospel with them. Since Cornelius had gathered many relatives, friends, and servants at his home in order to meet Peter, he was overjoyed at such acceptance.

You may disagree with their lifestyles, their morals, their principles, their religious beliefs, but the love required to fuel the big, spacious life modeled by Jesus always invites others to the party. If we're honest, none of us are going to agree on everything all the time. We can only agree on the one name with the power to save our souls: Jesus Christ.

Often the more you invite others in, the more you widen your circle—then the more your potential for disagreement increases. That's when it becomes crucial to remember what unites us. Our gathering is not built on agreement about anything but one—the name of Jesus, the name that is above every name.

Don't live in a world full of disagreement, trying to prove yourself right all the time. Don't build your life simply around others who agree with you all the time. Don't exclude others just because they disagree with you on many things. Such strife smells of and breeds disunity. Instead, allow the sweet aroma of the gospel to draw others to you and into the House of God, where they may also meet the One who saved you.

The Command to Love

Who we are and how we behave matters—it matters a great deal. Think about how the behavior and conduct of others either positively or negatively impacts you. Maybe you can recall a particular teacher at school who took the time to affirm you, giving you the courage to believe in yourself. Perhaps there was a pastor or mentor who went the extra mile to help you achieve your dream. You may also have memories of someone who spoke or acted cruelly toward you, making you feel insignificant or use-less. We should never underestimate the power we have over one another, especially the power of our leadership decisions over those who look to us for direction or support. It's not as though we have to be a perfect person to qualify in life—not at all—but we must be honest and teachable and live with authenticity and embrace others.

Jesus said, "'Love the Lord your God with all your passion and prayer and intelligence.' This is the most important, the first on any list. But there is a second to set alongside it: 'Love others as well as you love yourself.' These two commands are pegs; everything in God's Law and the Prophets hangs from them" (Matt. 22:37–40 MSG).

Heart Wide Open

Today we are called to love the people who perhaps historically the Church has never reached. We are called to love all people with the love of Christ, because his Father loves all people, wants to bless all people, and wants to save all people. I never want to be one of those people whose attitude and body language convey condemnation, judgment, and condescension. I want to be someone with arms wide open, heart wide open, and mind wide open to loving the people around me.

There is nobody who doesn't deserve to walk into their local church and have others look them in the eye and understand that we are all in the same position. We are all sinful, flawed, selfish, imperfect people—saved only by the grace of God and the love of Christ and the power of the Holy Spirit.

We don't have to agree, but we do have to invite them in. The

Church is not called to be an enforcer of rules but an outpost of grace. You and I are called to be dispensers of God's grace, purveyors of love, both inside and outside the church. It must be the tone of our lives.

God has no favorites, shows no partiality, and values no individual, group, or nation over another. While we want to love with the same all-inclusive embrace as our savior, the reality is that we often fall short.

I'm convinced we have to keep our hearts open before God and ask him to deal with us, to keep us compassionate, merciful, loving, and aware of the grace we've been given. When we live out of the fullness of this awareness of God's grace in our lives, then we are compelled to show it and to share it with others. May we always be people who understand the power of the gospel and understand that God has no favorites. You're his favorite. I'm his favorite—just as the drunk or the street worker down the road is his favorite. We are all his favorites.

You can enjoy the abundant life filled with the loving presence of your Father and in turn share the unlimited resources of his love with everyone you encounter. With Jesus as our example, we who have been given grace are called to shine it into a dark world. He said, "A new commandment I give to you, that you love one another; as I have loved you, that you also love one another. By this all will know that you are My disciples, if you have love for one another" (John 13:34–35).

Unconditional, inclusive love fuels the big life we long to live.

CHAPTER FIVE

Pioneering

Through waters uncharted my soul will embark.
I'll follow Your voice straight into the dark.
Should there come a moment when faith and I part,
Speak to the sails of my wandering heart.

"Captain," Hillsong Music, 2015

My pastor swings on a rope like a monkey."

Not exactly the words that you think would frame someone's salvation. And yet it was those words that drew some of our first converts into the House of God and triggered the ongoing blessing of thousands of people finding Jesus Christ at the altars of Hillsong Church.

I remember driving out to the farmlands of northwest Sydney over thirty years ago, looking out to the brown and dry landscape that was the Hills District at the time. The Hills were famous for only one thing: one of the most profitable and successful car dealerships in our nation, with an owner who would famously yell through people's television screens, *"Just up the Windsor Road from Baulkham Hills, and let me do it right for you!"* Driving by this dealership on the rural fringe of the city, I thought to myself, "If people are going to come out here in great numbers to buy a car…why wouldn't they come out here to attend a church?" Despite the bewildered looks I got from others, I was determined to build a church in this community—by God's grace, I could see what others couldn't.

On our very first Sunday, I was so encouraged as Bobbie and I looked around the little school hall that we had rented and counted seventy people. Seventy people in the Hills District on our first Sunday! My excitement was short-lived as the next week we had sixty-five, then fifty-three, then forty-five; I did the math and worked out that we had only four or five more weeks before we had no more people!

I was twenty-nine years old, young and carefree, and after that first month of trying to build from the ground up, one Sunday during my message—either out of excitement or desperation—I grabbed hold of one of two gymnastic ropes hanging from the school ceiling. I swung out over the congregation (which wasn't hard; they only went back a few rows), and there was a young man among the forty-five people there that day who found it so amusing.

The following week he went out and spoke to his friends, telling them, "You guys ought to come to my church—the pastor swings on a rope like a monkey!" The next week, he brought nine friends into the House of God, and all nine of them made commitments to Christ. The next week, they brought eleven more, and the following week, ten more. In three weeks he led thirty people to the saving grace of Jesus, and started a revival of passion in our little school hall. Little did he know that he was a pioneer.

A Pioneering Spirit

When we think of the word *pioneer* today, we might immediately think of Amelia Earhart, Capt. James Cook, Christopher Columbus, Albert Einstein, Steve Jobs, and countless others who have changed the face of history with their courageous and curious spirit. Their lives were dedicated to discovery and forward movement. Walt Disney, one of the twentieth century's most imaginative pioneers, once said of his growing empire, "Around here we don't look backwards for very long. We keep moving forward, opening up new doors and doing new things, because we're curious...and curiosity keeps leading us down new paths."

These new paths didn't always lead him to the success that is so often associated with the Disney name. In fact, in 1927 when Walt tried to get MGM studios to distribute Mickey Mouse, he was told that the idea would never work—they said a giant mouse on the screen would terrify women and children.

Pioneering takes courage, ingenuity, and a sense of adventure. With a pioneer spirit must come willingness to fail and falter, but with an unwavering belief in the long-term future vision. Pioneering doesn't come without its opposition, but the wide-open, spacious life we are seeking will undoubtedly require us to take some risks, step out of what is known, and count the cost of present comfort versus future reward. I believe it is God's will that we all have a pioneering spirit!

Starting Small, Dreaming Big

When you walk with Jesus, you never stop being a pioneer. This continues to prove true in my own life. I've been pioneering churches and pioneering in my life for over thirty years, and by God's grace I have never lost the pioneer spirit. When Bobbie and I moved to Australia in 1978, five years before we first began Hillsong Church, we pioneered a small church in a coastal area north of Sydney.

After a few months, it felt like the right time to hand that church on to another pastor, and shortly after that we were asked if we would consider taking on a church in Sydney's South-west. This church was in a desperate state. The congregation was made up of three old ladies, the church itself met in an old building in a rough area, and their only asset was a dilapidated old minibus in the front driveway. When we arrived, I looked around to see a pulpit that was bigger than I was, and more plastic flowers throughout the sanctuary than I'd seen in my lifetime. Well, I removed the pulpit and the plastic flowers, and wouldn't you know…two of the three congregation members left! Yet, as we began to make some changes and ask God for wisdom, the church began to grow and new life sprung forth from it.

From there we began what is now known as Hillsong Church. I remember distinctly some of our early days of ministry—we were young and adventurous and desperate for God to work through us. Arriving early with a few volunteers, we would set up the little school hall where we met, and stay late to pack it down. We borrowed baseball caps to make up for forgotten offering containers, and the dusty broom cupboard was our preservice meeting room. I look back now and thank God that other people in our world caught our pioneering spirit.

The Bible tells us, "Do not despise the day of small beginnings" (see Zech. 4:10). I believe that whatever it is God has entrusted into your hand—your family, your career, your ministry—don't count it as insignificant and don't approach it with a lack of vision. In the eyes of God and with his leading, wisdom, favor, and provision—if you hold fast to that which he has placed in your heart and do it with a pioneering spirit, I believe you will see it come to pass.

Taking New Territory

There are big things to be done with that raw-edged pioneering spirit as we live our lives both collectively as a church and individually. Based on the model of loving leadership we see in Christ, a pioneer takes territory previously considered uninhabitable and realizes its potential. Jesus always saw below the surface of people and knew what was in their hearts. He blazed a trail beyond human prejudices, biases, and stereotypes, and he calls his followers to do the same.

We see this when Philip takes the gospel message to Samaria, a place looked down upon by the Jews, because the region was inhabited not only by Gentiles but by Jewish people who had mixed with Gentiles. These people were seen as having compromised their heritage and were consequently viewed as outsiders, inferiors.

And yet there was Philip heading off to this undesirable area to be a pioneer of grace. Suddenly what had been viewed as uninhabitable and unreachable became a vital part of God's kingdom.

In fact, as the gospel spread among the Gentiles, it was no longer only the Jews who were chosen by God. Because of what Christ did for us on the cross, you and I can be part of the family of God.

We still have so many people to touch with God's love in our lives today. Whether it's someone you know a few doors down who dresses differently and practices another faith, or the homeless teen asking for change on the corner, outsiders have never gone away. We may have mapped our planet many times over, but we still have new territories of faith to explore.

Jesus consistently sought out people on the fringe of society, the individuals others dismissed. He talked to foreigners, women with bad reputations, men with deadly diseases, and children who wanted his attention. He refused to play the power games of the religious leaders of his day, leaving them frustrated and angry.

In Acts we see that his first disciples followed the same pattern. It was probably uncomfortable, inconvenient, and uncertain, but they obeyed the Lord's command to share the gospel of grace with all people, not just their Jewish neighbors. Christ destroyed the barriers of exclusion and the walls of elitism that many self-righteous Jews had constructed for themselves, and now his followers pioneered the wide-open territory left in his wake.

Consider that the first three individuals outside of Jerusalem whose lives were transformed by the gospel were not only outsiders but *way* outsiders. The first was a sorcerer, a wizard named Simon who confounded people with his magic tricks.

The second one (in Acts 8) was an Ethiopian eunuch. He was not only African, from a different county and culture, but he had been castrated, most likely to serve as a servant to the women, probably wives and concubines, of a rich man's household.

Regardless of his job, this man was definitely part of a small minority of outsiders.

And the third was Saul, who's described in the Bible as "breathing threats and murder" against Christians (Acts 9:1). He's also described as being in full agreement with the apostle Stephen being stoned and murdered for his faith. Yet Saul, this assassin of the Christian faith, ended up having a dramatic encounter with God while traveling on the road to the city of Damascus. He was literally blinded by the encounter and so dazed and disoriented that he didn't know what hit him. But gradually he realized the power of God's grace that he'd experienced, and he became a new man. He went from being the angry assailant Saul to being the humble yet powerful apostle Paul. Yes, the same Paul who wrote the many letters collected in the New Testament!

So a former wizard, a eunuch, and a hit man—how's that for an encouraging front row in church? Sounds more like the setup for some kind of joke! Clearly, the gospel is for everyone, not just Jewish religious leaders or the wealthy or successful. All backgrounds, all situations, all ethnicities are welcome in God's family. Just as Philip dared to step into unknown territory, we are God's pioneers, called to go beyond our comfort zones as we advance his kingdom.

Pioneering the Impossible

Pioneering by grace is in the DNA of Hillsong Church. In 1977 my parents, who were then in their midfifties, moved from New Zealand to Sydney, Australia. They went to the eastern suburbs and found a little hall in Double Bay, where they started a church they called Eastern Suburbs Christian Life Centre. As the church grew and moved to other sites, this building continued to serve a variety of purposes. When I drove by it recently, I noticed it now has LOCAL HISTORY CENTER painted across its doors, which seems fitting since it's where, in many ways, Hillsong actually started.

It was many years later, in 1999, when Bobbie and I were given the opportunity to do something that for us at that time was a bold and innovative step. We were asked to take on the leadership of my parents' inner-city church in addition to Hillsong, the church we were already pastoring in the northwest of Sydney. Although today there are countless models of incredible multisite churches, back in 1999 it was totally new territory, and we had no role models to look to for guidance. We were pioneers.

Sixteen years on, our City Campus is a thriving and integral part of Hillsong Church. Along the way we have learned a great deal about multisite expansion and global church planting, as Hillsong has spread to some of the world's most influential cities. I am not called to plant churches everywhere, but where we do, my hope and prayer is that we can build significant churches whose impact for the Cause of Christ spreads far beyond their own walls and welcomes everyone.

From the very beginning, we've always endeavored to be a pioneering church, not always having to do new things, but finding God doing fresh things as we've worked to hear his voice and follow his leading. It hasn't always been the easy road—sometimes it's been the costly one—but pioneering in the will of God has ultimately brought about great eternal fruit and reward.

Dr. Elmer Towns of Liberty University has recently written a book titled *The Ten Most Influential Churches of the Past Century*. I was surprised and honored that he included Hillsong in his selection. Dr. Towns states: "Hillsong Church, Sydney, Australia, may not be the very first to use contemporary praise-music, but the church not only pioneered the movement in Australia, it became the lead church in teaching the church to worship the Lord in contemporary praise music."[1]

Thirty years ago, with seventy people in our first service in a school hall in the suburbs of Sydney, we would have laughed at the idea of being influential. I bet that young man who brought thirty friends to church with him had no idea what the eternal impact of his decisions would be. We haven't tried to be pioneers for the sake of recognition or novelty or fame. Over many years we have simply endeavored to build Christ's church and see people connect with Jesus, be discipled in his truth, and grow in God's purposes for their lives. I believe this is what it means to lead a big life: pioneering by following Christ's example.

Pioneer Your Present Territory

Jesus himself was the ultimate pioneer. He did what no one had ever done before or has done since: died for our sins and rose from the dead. He is the essence of what it means to live in your grace zone, to embrace what you've been given by God and extend it to the adventure of life you're called to explore.

By definition, a pioneer is one of the first or among the earliest explorers in any field of enterprise or progress. A pioneer stretches boundaries and extends horizons. A pioneer sings a song that is music to the uninitiated, to those lost in the wilderness behind him. A pioneer defies the odds again and again,

---

1. Towns, Elmer L. *The Ten Most Influential Churches of the Past Century* (Shippensburg, PA: Destiny Image).

repeatedly taking risks and bringing longevity and completion to his pursuits.

If you want to follow Jesus, to walk with him closely and experience the power of his love, then you must be a pioneer, a passionate leader in the exploration of the uncharted wilderness of your spacious life. Now you may not think of yourself as a leader, let alone a pioneer, based on the way our world and culture defines them. But if you follow Jesus, then you are a pioneering leader. You may not recognize the authority and resources you've been given, others may not recognize your leadership, but if you have the Holy Spirit living in you, then God has anointed you as a leader in his revolution to free every human being from the slavery of sin.

You don't have to be elected to office or rule governments, amass real estate, or build huge businesses. You may not oversee companies or guide industries, you may not chair the board or command the team, but if you're following Jesus Christ, then you are called to take a stand and to serve his kingdom. It is our mandate to exercise the talents and abilities that we have been given so that God's kingdom will grow and other people's lives will be changed.

We are each called to lead our lives in a way pleasing to God, in a manner that fulfills our divine potential, whether we're called to hold earthly positions of authority or not. Whether you are the leader of a global company, the leader of a Bible study at church, or simply a leader in your home with your children—you are a pioneer in your present territory!

What big discovery have you missed that's waiting right around the corner? Where are you continuing to search for God's guidance as you apply your talents and steward the resources you've been given? If we ever lose that pioneering spirit, I wonder what enormous surprise we will never know we missed out on this side of eternity. What is it that is in your hand right now that requires courage, tenacity, maybe a bit of risk, and the spirit of a pioneer?

No matter where you find yourself in life right now, it's not too late. Praise God, we have that same opportunity in our lives today, to believe God and to see new opportunities for growth, new possibilities for fulfilling our potential.

The big life we long to live can so often be hijacked by setbacks or stumbles, unexpected bumps in the road. But if we spend our time looking to or dwelling on the past, we may never meet the God appointment waiting for us in the future. Nothing is impossible for the One who has called you, sent you, and promises to do the journey with you.

It's time you look at life with the spirit of a pioneer.

PART 2

A Difficult Path

CHAPTER SIX

The Worst Day of My Life

Christ alone, Cornerstone. Weak made strong in
the Saviour's love.
Through the storm, He is Lord. Lord of All.
                    "Cornerstone," Hillsong Music, 2012

It's not about you—it's about your father."

These words introduced me to a nightmare that would ultimately continue to unfold over all the ensuing years of my life. I was forty-five years old at the time, and what developed next after that sentence was a product of someone else's past that would frame so much of my future.

It was late in October 1999, and George Aghajanian, my friend with whom I've worked for many, many years, sat across from me for our weekly Tuesday meeting. As general manager of Hillsong Church, George oversees most of the staff and all administrative functions for us on a global scale. He always comes prepared with a list of items we need to discuss, often beginning with simple matters we can check off quickly and working his way up to more serious concerns that may require some discussion.

So on that October day, springtime in Australia, we sat in my office at the Hills Campus of Hillsong Church going over

George's list. We moved through most items quickly, and I actually thought we might wrap up a bit early. In fact, I suspect my mind may have already started to drift a bit, looking ahead at my next appointments and wondering if I might get in a quick jog. But then George looked at me and said, "There's just one more thing, Brian."

"Go on," I said and nodded for him to continue. He hesitated, and I sensed he had something important to tell me. I could tell almost immediately by his tone and the serious look in his eyes that whatever he was about to tell me was not going to be good news.

"It's not about you," he said. "It's about your father."

My heart pounded in my chest, and it felt as if all the blood drained from my face. George then proceeded to tell me how a phone call had come into our church office. The caller told one of our pastors that he had recently been ministering at a local church and that after his talk, a lady asked to speak with him. It was during this conversation that she exposed to him something (I later learned) she had been carrying for many years: "Frank Houston sexually abused my son."

Of all the things that George might have told me about my father, this could not have been further from what I had expected to hear. In fact, I didn't even have a category for this kind of accusation. While I'm sure it was only a matter of seconds, time seemed frozen as a riptide of painful emotions washed over me, wave after wave. Confusion. Anger. Incredulity. Fear. Hurt. Betrayal.

To give you some context, my father—William Francis "Frank" Houston—had always been my hero. Some of my earliest memories date back to attending tent revival meetings with him in the far north of New Zealand. Entire valleys and villages of beautiful Maori people, New Zealand's native inhabitants, were being saved as my father preached the good news of the gospel, night after night. During the day, the Waiomio locals would teach my brother and me how to ride horses, and in the late afternoon we would stand just on the cusp of the river, catching eels by flicking them between our legs and onto the banks. Our newfound friends would cook up our catch and introduce us to the delicacies of their culture. My childhood was filled with memories of waving good-bye to my dad as he took off on yet another ministry trip—and as I watched him longingly I remember believing that I, too, would do just that one day. So much of my motivation for wanting to serve God and build the church came from my father. Which is why the very thought of this story was so shattering.

We never like thinking about the private lives of our parents, but to consider the things George was saying about my dad—things that seemed so out of character for the man who had raised me, loved me, and taught me so much about God and the ministry—was, to say the least, *unbelievable*.

The thought that my father, who was then in his late seventies, would commit such a heinous act as sexual abuse was crippling. As details of the allegations unfolded in my office that day, within seconds I realized that it wasn't only abuse against another male, it was someone underage, a child. Someone who, along with his family, looked up to my dad who was a prominent pastor in New Zealand when this incident happened in the late 1960s or early 1970s, and was a visitor to Sydney at the time. This was several years before my parents had actually moved to Australia and pioneered Sydney Christian Life Centre, and Hillsong Church did not exist back then. My mind quickly moved from the facts, to recognition that this happened to a young boy who was not even ten years old at the time, and I thought to myself, "This is not just immoral—it's criminal." My father had committed pedophilia. In fact, it dawned on me in these moments that I myself was only a youth at the time of these events. These thoughts began overwhelming me as I processed the reality of what was happening.

What started as just another Tuesday, a good day to be alive, suddenly became the worst day of my life. And little did I know how much worse it would get…

The Silent Crash

I think in life, especially as people of faith, we believe for the best. But let's be honest: If you live long enough, we will all have those days when we hear the worst. It could be the call in the middle of the night—never good news—about the health of an aging parent or from the police who have just arrested your teenage child. It could be a conversation with your boss, one that you thought was going to be a regular appointment that suddenly turns into your job's termination. It could be a routine checkup revealing something more serious, or a knock at your door resulting in a court summons in your hand.

I always try to live with an expectation for the best, but it's true that we never know what our worst day will be, or when it will be. Life is seasonal. The Bible virtually promises us that "in this world, we will have trouble" (see John 16:33). No matter how big and spacious our lives may be, how successful, wealthy, educated, or smart we are, we all encounter detours on the path of life that leave us in the ditch, things that blindside us, events we could never anticipate, secrets exposed we could never imagine.

This was certainly the case with the news about my dad. At the time the accusations came to light, I was not only pastor of our growing church, I was also president of a denomination with over 1,100 churches. So my mind was spinning after that conversation with George. Even though these crimes had occurred decades earlier, back when I was in my teens and obviously unaware, somehow deep down in my heart, I knew that I was about to find out that these accusations were in fact true. The possibility did, and the truth still does, make my stomach sick. There's not too much worse than finding out that your father is a pedophile. You couldn't have thrown something less expected and more devastating at me.

My father was overseas at the time of my meeting with George, which gave me a little time to gather my thoughts and seek more information in preparation for the hardest conversation I've ever had. On the Tuesday after he returned, my dad came into my office for what he thought was a routine meeting. I tried to stay as calm as I could and outlined to him the call we'd received. I remember he had just come back from overseas and already looked tired. But then as he heard my statement, he seemed to age before my very eyes. How do you talk to your father, who is also your hero, about something so horrible? There was a long and difficult pause and then he began to speak, his mouth going all dry as he admitted that yes, the accusation I was relaying to him was true.

As president of our denomination, it was my responsibility then and there to suspend him from ministry and ask for his credentials. I believe he left my office that day knowing that he would never preach again—and he never did.

At that time, my father told me it had only happened once. While I definitely prayed that this was true, I knew that the future had suddenly become very uncertain.

Knock It Off

Throughout the entire ordeal, I kept going only because I knew God was with me. I had to rely on his power to face a situation that was personally and professionally beyond my imagination. Yet, more than all the professional and personal pain, I also lived with the awareness that there was someone out there who was hurting so much more than I—an innocent victim whose life had also been forever changed. During this time I just knew I couldn't bear the pain by myself and remain the leader God had called me to be for our church and denomination. I needed my Heavenly Father.

Jesus handled his own suffering this same way, drawing his strength from his Father's power. And it must have been so much harder for him because, as the Son of God, he absolutely had the ability to change the situation he faced. When the worst happens to you and me, we don't have the option to snap our fingers and make it go away, but Jesus could have. And yet he chose not to take the easy way out. Instead he chose to suffer and die as an innocent man so that all people, who certainly deserve punishment for their sins, could be forgiven and live forever.

However, Jesus was also fully human and apparently wrestled with how to handle the difficult path ahead of him. We see this in the conversation he had with his disciples in Matthew 16. It is in this conversation that Jesus' disciples told him that some believed him to be John the Baptist or Elijah or one of the other prophets of generations past. And then Christ asked them who they thought he was. Peter answered correctly—that Jesus was indeed the Messiah, God's Son sent to earth to save his people.

Since it's not time for Jesus to reveal his identity publicly, however, he told his disciples to keep quiet.

But he also told them about the difficult path that lay ahead of him. Jesus told them that he had to go to Jerusalem and face the wrath of the many hypocritical Jewish religious leaders before being arrested and executed and then raised from the dead on the third day. If the disciples knew the Old Testament prophecies about the Messiah, and most if not all probably did, then they realized that Jesus did not have an easy time ahead. This painful vision of the future upset Peter so much he took his Master aside and basically said, "No! This can't happen to you—you're the Son of God! I don't want this to happen and will not allow it."

Jesus responded to Peter's outburst with a very dramatic exclamation of his own. "Get behind me, Satan!" He called his beloved friend, and the man he had earlier called the rock upon which he would build his church, the worst thing I can think of—Satan! This may seem a bit extreme at first glance. After all, surely Peter had not secretly pledged his allegiance to the devil so that he could be a spy and tempt Christ into avoiding what he was about to face. We might even expect Jesus to respond to Peter kindly: "Thank you for your concern, Peter. I know you mean well and don't want me to have to face the suffering ahead, but that's why I'm here on earth—to save mankind from their sins."

Instead he gives a fiery pushback. Jesus told his disciple that he was offensive, a "stumbling block," as the New International Version translates it (Matt. 16:23), more mindful of earthly things than the ways of God. That's quite an indictment! But one that clearly reflects Jesus' humanity. I think he basically said, "Look,

Peter, this is hard enough! Don't tempt me to use my divine power to avoid all the painful events that I have to endure. You're trying to plant ideas in my head about how to avoid suffering. You're trying to get me to limit my view of God's plan and focus only on my own comfort. But that's shortsighted. So knock it off!"

We face the same temptation but have to keep our eyes on Jesus.

He didn't take a detour around the shadowed valley ahead.

So we must follow him through it.

Your Own Revelation

Whenever the path grows difficult for us, whenever we enter the valley of the shadow and feel as if the worst has happened, it is easy to struggle with being shortsighted and earthly minded. Just as Jesus called out Peter as being of the devil for tempting him to take an easy way out, I believe such thoughts originate from the same place of fear. We can't imagine how we'll get through such a painful ordeal, so we want to take the first way out we see. We don't want to have to suffer, uncertain of when— or if—we will come out the other side.

However, in my mind, I knew I had no option but to confront this—I had to walk the difficult path before me.

From that day of confession, it was my responsibility to speak to the elders of Sydney Christian Life Centre, and begin what was a horrific and yet necessary series of conversations and events that brought these revelations to light. In the days to come, and as soon as it became practically possible, our national executives also gathered in a boardroom, and as forthright as I could be,

I bluntly communicated the devastating news to everyone around the table. I handed the chair of the meeting to someone else, and I sat as the wise men, who had so many times before served my vision and watched my father lead, began to talk about a way forward.

Twelve months later, more accusations began to emerge of abuse that had occurred in the same time frame, back in New Zealand, at the hands of my father—several of them proving to be true. As painful as it was—and still is—God promised to remain by my side throughout this dark valley of desperate days.

Knowing that I had to trust in him like never before, I committed to facing the truth and doing what had to be done, no matter how painful. The fallout in my family alone was immense. My siblings addressed their own pain in various ways as they struggled to come to grips with the knowledge that the loving dad they always knew was a man with evil secrets.

The things he did were wrong, terrible, and shocking. But the only way that I knew how to move forward was to endure the pain of this difficult season.

Navigating this situation publicly, as a highly visible pastor, I also had to process this devastating news on a personal level. As a husband and a father, and as a son. I had to talk to my kids about their granddad, who was much beloved and an absolute hero to all of us.

I'll never forget when I talked to each of my kids to tell them this devastating news. They all responded differently, but in my mind they responded so incredibly well. Ben, my second son, now the pastor of Hillsong Los Angeles, listened carefully as a seventeen-year-old and tried to take it all in. After we shared a few moments of silence together, I said, "Ben, I so hope this doesn't affect your faith."

He nodded and said, "Don't worry, Dad. That's not going to happen—I've had my own revelation of Jesus." At the time those were the most golden words I could have heard. Each of us must cling to our own revelation of Jesus whenever bleak days try to obscure our faithful path.

My father never ministered again, and he descended quickly into old age as the shame and torment of his dark past overtook him. Five years later, suffering from dementia, and only ten months after my mother passed away, my father had an apparent stroke in the shower—fell backward, hit his head, and died. My disgraced hero was gone.

I find myself now reliving the realities of that day in 1999 and still dealing with and navigating the effects of such a difficult journey. Yet I have learned that when we walk through the valley of the shadow, when we turn a corner and glimpse a difficult path filled with pain and heartache ahead, we can only go forward.

And in order to take the next step forward and then the next, we must lean on God and keep our eyes on Jesus. He has promised never to leave us or forsake us and will guide us through our darkest days. So that even in the valley of the shadow, with God on our side we can proclaim: "Surely goodness and mercy shall follow me all the days of my life; and I will dwell in the house of the LORD forever" (Ps. 23:6).

CHAPTER SEVEN

Understanding the Process of Pain

This is my prayer in the desert,
when all else within me feels dry,
this is my prayer in my hunger and need,
my God is the God who provides.

"Desert Song," Hillsong Music, 2008

Whenever I think about the way life can suddenly tilt into a crisis, I recall one of the great heroes of Australia, Capt. James Cook. Now there was a pioneer. In 1770 he sailed into beautiful Botany Bay, one of three beautiful harbors that form the backdrop of what is now the city of Sydney, along the east coast of Australia's mainland. He is generally considered the person who discovered Australia, though unfortunately he discovered it the hard way. No one told Captain Cook about the Great Barrier Reef, a twelve-hundred-mile shelf of beautiful but jagged coral and one of the world's great wonders. And as you might suspect, jagged coral and his old wooden ship, the *Endeavour*, didn't get along very well. So Captain Cook got caught on the reef in a perilous situation and his ship began to sink.

If not for the quick thinking of his resourceful crew, who began to throw objects overboard to lighten their weight, the *Endeavour* would have fallen into a watery grave. But crew members threw over everything they could get their hands on—ballasts, tools, jars of olives, bags of grain, even their cannons. They tossed all sorts of things overboard in order to survive. Eventually, their ship became light enough to float above the reef and continue to sail. The spot where they got stuck, however, has become rather famous. And guess what it's called? Cape Tribulation!

We all have our Cape Tribulations. Scripture even tells us that such trials are inevitable. "To *everything* there is a season, a time for *every purpose* under heaven" (Ecc. 3:1; emphasis added). As much as we may not like it or understand it, *everything* means all the painful, unexpected, disappointing, frightening, challenging moments as well as all the joyful, predictable, exciting, reassuring, and comfortable ones. Life includes times of pain, of mourning and grieving, of suffering and healing, and of fighting and reconciling.

The greater problem may be when we get stuck in our pain, when we can't seem to find the strength to get back on our feet and continue our journey. Life is a difficult path, but it keeps going. If we stop just because we're in pain and can't imagine how to continue, then we will miss out on what God wants to do in our lives. I don't believe that suffering itself is from God, but I believe he uses our suffering—because with him, nothing is wasted. With Christ as our model for living, loving, and leading, we see that he suffered beyond what we can imagine so that we can enjoy the reality of eternal life:

> He is despised and rejected by men,
> a Man of sorrows and acquainted with grief.

And we hid, as it were, our faces from Him;
He was despised, and we did not esteem Him.

Surely He has borne our griefs
And carried our sorrows;
yet we esteemed Him stricken,
Smitten by God, and afflicted.
But He was wounded for our transgressions,
He was bruised for our iniquities;
the chastisement for our peace was upon Him,
And by His stripes we are healed. (Isaiah 53:3–5)

We have a Savior who not only knows what it means to suffer but who willingly gave himself as a sacrifice in our place. He loved us enough to take more than a bullet for us—he took the cross. And he defeated sin and death so that we can have grace and joy and hope. Because Christ rose from the dead, we can endure the trials that come our way on life's difficult path. But like Captain Cook's crew aboard their sinking ship, we often have to lighten our load if we want to keep sailing.

Learning My Limits

I learned this lesson, about letting go of the heavy weights bearing down on me, the hard way. Although I handled the situation with my dad as best I could, relying on the power of God's Spirit to give me the courage, strength, and stamina to keep going, the ongoing pain took its toll. When my father passed away in 2004, I grieved for the dad I had known growing up: the loving man who was my hero and role model; the brilliant preacher and

evangelist, the man who gathered crowds and had them screaming hilariously with laughter one moment and weeping the next,
as he told incredible stories of faith. And I struggled to come to
terms with the realities of the man that I never knew, the one
who harbored dark struggles himself and committed acts I could
never have imagined. This, too, kept the pain alive in my body
and in my heart.

Finally, I reached a point where the cumulative impact of all
the stress, strife, and struggle became too much for me. Over the
next twelve years, after that initial conversation about my father
with George in my office, I found myself in a downward slide
toward depression, traumatized by the experience years earlier and
internally declining as I tried to look after everyone but myself.
Outwardly, my life was exploding. Our church was flourishing in
Australia and taking off globally, the impact of Hillsong Music
was on the rise, our television ministry was experiencing unprecedented growth, and God was affording Bobbie and me a growing influence over our kingdom endeavors. And yet internally I
was imploding.

With growth came a level of scrutiny that we had never experienced before. I felt removed from my life, from the passion
and purpose that usually kept me eager to get out of bed in
the morning and greet the day ahead. I was going through the
motions, often lost in my thoughts, uncertain how to regain my
joy and peace.

I was traveling an enormous amount during this time, ministering abroad and building our global campuses. With the
frequent time changes and opportunity to sleep on airplanes,
I found myself taking a sleeping tablet to catch a few hours of
rest or simply to get over jet lag. It didn't take long before the

tablets lost their effectiveness, and I began to take more than one in order to reap their intended benefit. A number of years later, I found I could no longer get any restful sleep without taking a sleeping pill.

My family noticed and began to ask me if I was okay. I told them I was and tried to keep going as long as I could, preaching and speaking, traveling and leading, as Hillsong continued to grow and God continued to do amazing things. However, the physical toll of this period of unrest began to manifest as my mind became scattered, and I wasn't speaking with the same confidence I had experienced in ministry years earlier. God was gracious to me because despite my personal challenges, people were still experiencing blessing and finding freedom in Christ in our church; yet those closest to me knew all was not well with my soul.

Then one day something collapsed within me. It was as if all the emotional strength in my tank had suddenly been drained. My ship was sinking, weighed down by excess baggage and other issues of life, and I found myself shattered on a great reef of jagged pain, fear, and sorrow. Bobbie and I were visiting our beachside campus of N̲ ̲ ̲ ̲ ̲ ̲utiful Queensland, after a whirlwind ̲ ̲ ̲ ̲ ̲ ̲ ̲ ̲g Conferences and traveling across ̲ ̲ ̲ ̲ ̲ ̲ed to speak that Sunday night, and a̲ ̲ ̲ ̲ ̲ ̲message I felt physically weak, and m̲ ̲ ̲ ̲ ̲d toward the podium. My words wer̲ ̲ ̲ ̲ ̲aking gibberish—and it felt more like ̲ ̲ ̲ ̲day school message rather than a sermon.

As we arrived back at our room later that night, I found myself in a state of fear and panic while thinking on the stresses of life, and I suddenly began struggling for air. I couldn't breathe normally and felt my heart jackhammer faster and faster inside of my chest. I began to sweat and my mouth went dry. A million thoughts raced through my mind at once, but I couldn't open my mouth to explain them. Breathless and fearful, I felt like I was suffocating, and I exclaimed to Bobbie that I thought perhaps I was going to die.

It was after midnight at the time, and Bobbie knew immediately I was having a panic attack. Luckily, she was able to get a hold of a faithful member of our congregation, a doctor who was able to talk me through this episode on the telephone and was eager to see me as soon as we arrived back in Sydney. Eventually, I was diagnosed with Posttraumatic Stress Disorder (PTSD), and other doctors suggested that I might continue to have panic attacks for my whole life, but I determined in my heart that was not going to happen.

The diagnosis made sense from a logical, clinical perspective, and in some ways I was relieved because all of a sudden everything that I was experiencing felt validated. Yet in some ways I was very shocked. Surely the doctors weren't talking about me! I had always been strong enough to handle everything; I was never "that guy" who buckled under pressure. I grew up happy-go-lucky, remained a visionary, and was experiencing some levels of success. What was in my heart was growing, and I wanted to be the one others could lean on for support. I could not believe I had allowed my life to get to this point. Yet I had to come to terms with the fact that I wasn't invincible. Although my God is all-powerful, I am not. My body, mind, and spirit have limits.

Immediately I took a few days off to think on my priorities, and I changed the way I had been living and leading. I made some big decisions about the way I approached both travel and ministry, I stopped taking the sleeping tablets that were modifying my behavior and negatively impacting my emotions, and I let God take control of the stresses that were weighing me down. During this time I knew there were many people praying—I have always been blessed with an incredibly loving and supportive family. By the grace of God, I bounced back quickly. I have never had another panic attack and expect I never will. This bump in the road was unexpected, but with the help of my family, trusted counsel, and the peace of God, it didn't sink my ship.

Despite how painful your circumstances may be, no matter how difficult life's path may seem, you will not be destroyed. I believe life is all about choices, and we can choose to cooperate with the words of death and sickness spoken over our lives, or we can choose to rise above them. The anguish you feel is real, but there's something more powerful, more potent, more all-encompassing than any loss, crisis, or trauma we can encounter: the love of God through the power of his Son, Jesus Christ.

> For I am persuaded that neither death nor life, nor angels nor principalities nor powers, nor things present nor things to come, nor height nor depth, nor any other created thing, shall be able to separate us from the love of God which is in Christ Jesus our Lord. (Romans 8:38–39)

No matter how difficult life's path, nothing can separate you from the love of God.

Process and Progress

While nothing can separate us from God's presence, in order to recover, heal, and grow stronger, we must understand the process of pain. While we wish it would go away tomorrow, most burdens don't just disappear the next morning. It's clear in the Bible that suffering and struggles are an ongoing process, not a onetime event or moment. When I think about my own experiences, I often want to progress out of my challenges without having to embrace the process. However, we must all realize that pain cannot be neatly compartmentalized and boxed away on a shelf. The painful events we suffer bleed into our lives every day if we ignore them.

We saw in Scripture how everything has a season and a time for every purpose under Heaven (Ecc. 3:1). So this means if every season has a purpose, then there's a process for that purpose to be worked out. We often feel as if we can't see any good purpose in the trials of life whatsoever, but it's amazing how God can use anything and everything to take you forward and actually make you a better person. To make you stronger, wiser, and more compassionate. To give your ministry a bit more depth, your business a new lease on life, your family a second chance at affection and understanding. To force you into his arms for a closer, more intimate relationship.

Though I have experienced trials since, internally my heart and soul remain steadfast. So, as much as we may want to, we can't ignore the importance of the process. I myself have learned to recognize and acknowledge the process of pain, and I've learned to cooperate with the answer rather than remain a victim to the problem.

In Scripture there are many examples to describe what happens when we don't wait on God's timing and embrace the process of painful circumstances. When we procrastinate and avoid the hard choices and difficult actions necessary to move through our pain, it usually results in calamity. Denial only compounds the pain and causes it to grow and fester like an infection in your body.

When our kids were small, like many young families we opted for road trips instead of costly flights. These lengthy journeys in the car undoubtedly rang with the familiar question from the backseat: "Are we there yet?" My kids recall my response with sarcastic humor now, but my consistent answer would always be "No...we have miles and miles to go!" There was no watering down the long road ahead, and my honest response was in a considered effort to toughen them up for the journey.

Our trials are similar. Don't delay what should be addressed at the beginning of the process in hopes that you can avoid it or somehow minimize your suffering. As excruciating as it feels at the time, doing the right thing and being obedient to God allows you to move through the process faster and more aware of what is to come.

Soul Supporter

Embracing the process does not mean wallowing in self-pity or relying on your own efforts to get you through the pain. We'll explore the role of relationships and the power of community on life's difficult path in the coming chapters, but for now let me just say that you must accept the fact that we all need support. When you're in the midst of a trial filled with turmoil and trauma, then you need the comfort of others, you need support, and you need God.

Earlier I mentioned how the Bible is filled with examples of how difficult life can be and the process of pain. Perhaps there's no better, more concentrated example of this truth than what we find throughout the Psalms. As you probably know, the Psalms are a collection of poems and song lyrics, many of them written by David, the shepherd boy who became king of Israel. Many of David's beautiful words reflect the joy and sheer wonder he experienced in his relationship with God. But many of them also reflect his anger, his pain, his grief, and his fear.

In Psalm 142, one of his rawest expressions, David begins by saying, "I cry out to the LORD with my voice; with my voice to the LORD I make my supplication. I pour out my complaint before Him; I declare before Him my trouble" (v. 1–2). From there, he launches into a bit of a laundry list about why he's feeling so down. Basically, he reveals just how low he feels with a sense that everyone's out to get him, setting snares for him, ignoring his pain, and not acknowledging his need for comfort. Such emotions can be common to us all: "Nobody cares about me." "That person is out to get me." "Why isn't anyone helping me?" "Woe is me!"

But then David concludes the Psalm by reminding himself of what he knows to be true: "Lord, you are my refuge!" (see Ps. 142:5). In fact, this theme and this very phrase occurs in many other Psalms, including 18, 46, 62, and 91. We must cry out to God, letting him know how overwhelmed we are with pain, with grief, with anger. I can't tell you how many times during the months and years after October 1999 that I withdrew emotionally or questioned the ways others handled my silent pain. Yet even when I wasn't sure I could handle it, I knew God could handle my pain. So like David, I cried out to him and reminded myself of what I knew to be true, even if I didn't particularly feel it in that moment.

God will *always* be your soul supporter.

Especially on your worst days.

Bring My Soul out of Prison

In Psalm 142, David declares, "Bring my soul out of prison, that I may praise Your name" (v. 7). As represented in Psalm 142, David does what we have to do in order to move through the process of pain that occurs when life gets difficult. He made a choice to surround himself with the righteous, and even though he began a Psalm with crying, he ended it with praising.

David's Psalm reminds me so much of a story within our own church, one that remains deeply personal for Bobbie and me. While my sons were in high school, they met another young man named Matt, or "Stealth," as all his mates called him. Stealth was a talented young swimmer and a bright student with so much drive and determination, the kind of friend you wanted for your sons. Yet the pain that he endured in his young life was more than most people could handle.

At a young age, Stealth was adopted into a wonderful family. His adoptive parents cared for him with extravagance, sending him to a good school and loving him and his siblings as their own. When he was in his early teens, Stealth's mum was diagnosed with cancer and quickly declined, passing away just after his seventeenth birthday. Only a few years later, his father also passed away, leaving Stealth and his siblings as orphans. He needed family, and it was our privilege to bring him into our world.

Stealth lived out his university days alongside my son Joel, and he was a fixture in our church—where he met one of our young Hillsong College students, Jill. Jill was from the United States, an incredibly talented young lady who served on our worship team as a leader and songwriter. Their romance developed quickly, until they were eventually married; and just two years after their wedding, they shared with us the excited news that they were expectant with their first child.

Max Kingston McCloghry was born at just twenty-three weeks gestation and went to be with Jesus on the same day. Matt told me of the friends who gathered at the hospital during those uncertain hours—joining them as they cried out to God on behalf of their friends and firstborn whose little life touched so many. The grief that Stealth had already experienced in his young life culminated that night in February as he and Jill wept over the son they had longed for and loved, only to be disappointed by such an unfair and unexplainable tragedy.

This was one of the hardest funerals I have ever had to preside over. Because of the love and respect we have for Stealth and Jill, Bobbie and I, along with our kids and our church family, wept that day as we said our good-byes. Yet I believe the events that unfolded over the next few weeks caused the pain and defeat of the circumstances to bow to the powerful healing and comfort that we have in Jesus.

It was only days after Baby Max's funeral, and we were not only hosting the 2008 annual Colour Conference, but also about to start recording the Hillsong Worship album, *This Is Our God*. Brooke Ligertwood was finishing the lyrics to a new song, and her relationship with Jill caused her to ask her friend—who was going through undoubtedly her darkest hour—if she would consider leading worship alongside her that night, only weeks after her loss. As Jill bravely took to the platform that evening, the sense of God's presence was so tangible. As many people would witness that night, as she sung, it was as if her soul was freed from the prison of her wounds, and that evening she led an entire stadium into an abandonment of worship like we had never known. She boldly declared:

> *All of my life, in every season,*
> *You are still God.*
> *I have a reason to sing, I have a reason to worship.*
> *"Desert Song," Hillsong Music, 2008*

Grief is a hard road, and one that is not to be diminished. Yet, many years on, still walking out their journey of healing (and being a blessing to many others who are walking theirs), Jill and Matt are raising two beautiful children, gifts from God, and living a big, wide-open life in New York City. Through the choices of people whose hearts were steadfast and in love with Jesus, and because of the unending grace of an Almighty God, what began as a prison of pain has become a prism of praise.

Peace Like a River

No matter who you are, or how many years you've been a Christian, everyone will come up against challenges and trials at times. But in these times you discover that the strength of your spirit and the health of your soul comes from God. Such setbacks do take a toll, and we look to both God and people for comfort, but the Bible tells us not to let the troubles of this world devastate you. "A healthy spirit conquers adversity, but what can you do when the spirit is crushed" (Prov. 18:14 MSG). Commit to going the distance with God, allowing his grace to carry you, empower you, and sustain you when you're overwhelmed and can't imagine how you'll keep going.

Sometimes I fear we get in the way of the supernatural healing God wants to give us in the midst of our pain. If I had fixed my thoughts only on what my dad did and all the terrible repercussions, then I would have indeed become paralyzed with sorrow, anger, and bitterness. So I had to keep my perspective focused on Christ. *What you focus on in life determines whether or not you will experience peace in your heart.* The Bible gives us clear instructions about finding and living in a place of peace, as well as what takes away our peace.

Anxiety and worry work in opposition to inner peace. When you are worried or anxious about something, even something that must be faced and embraced as a process, you leave little room for God's peace. As I have discovered, worrying is a genuine health hazard. The Bible tells us, "Anxiety in the heart of man causes depression, but a good word makes it glad" (Prov. 12:25) or as the New Living Translation renders it, "Worry weighs a person down; an encouraging word cheers a person up."

Peace will flow like a river if you don't allow your heart to harden and form a dam. I could do nothing to change what my father had done all those years ago. Jill and Matty had no control over the circumstances life threw at them. They simply had to focus on the present moving forward. Worrying is about trusting in your own ability and not resting in the faith of God's power and goodness. Scripture is undeniably clear: "Be anxious for nothing, but in everything by prayer and supplication, with thanksgiving, let your requests be made known to God; and the peace of God, which surpasses all understanding, will guard your hearts and minds through Christ Jesus" (Phil. 4:6–7).

If you want to live a big, spacious, abundant life like Jesus, especially when life gets difficult, then make the daily decision to believe God at his Word. Believe that his promise for you is for success as you sow the seeds of faith and patience. Ask God to help you be patient as you move through the process of pain and wait for his promises over your life to be fulfilled. Ask him to fill you with hope and trust, believing him to be a good God who desires good things for your life. And ask him to grant you the peace that's promised in his Word: "And the peace of God, which passeth all understanding, shall keep your hearts and minds through Christ Jesus" (Phil. 4:7 KJV).

The wide-open, spacious life is your portion—but oh, how unpredictable the path can be!

CHAPTER EIGHT

Shame, No More

**A thousand times I've failed, still Your mercy
remains,
and should I stumble again, still I'm caught in
Your grace.**
"From the Inside Out," Hillsong Music, 2006

When I was thirteen, my mum called both my siblings and me into the family room and told us she had a big surprise for us. She and Dad had agreed to take care of a baby for a while, sort of like foster parents, and she would need all of us to help. I was surprised along with the rest of my family, since this was the first we had heard of it. But sure enough, a couple weeks later, my mother brought this baby to our house and we looked after him for the following year.

What I didn't know at the time was that this baby was actually my nephew. My older sister, who was about seventeen at the time, had recently moved from Wellington, New Zealand, to Melbourne on the east coast of Australia. What we didn't know was that our parents had secreted her away when they found out she was pregnant out of wedlock. As pastors of a church, my parents were bearing the weight of guilt and shame associated with the mentality of the day, and they felt like they had little choice but to send her away. I later found out that she was sent across the channel to Australia for several months before quietly being brought back to a little town called Martinborough, just across the Rimutaka mountain range from our home. There she had the baby who came and spent his first year or so with us.

It was some time into this journey that I found out my sister's secret. In fact, I was rummaging through some drawers years later and found paperwork, only to realize the baby's mother was my sister! In that era, in that landscape, there was so much shame attached to unwed mothers, and she was made to feel the full brunt of it. Today, I'm sad to think about the idea of my sister quietly having a baby as a shameful secret rather than a wonderful blessing. It affected her for many years, but fortunately her story has a beautiful ending. Today, my nephew Rick and his mum and siblings enjoy a close family relationship.

I know my sister is not alone in having to battle a secret shame. So many people allow their actions to be poisoned by shame, and then it controls them. Shame robs you of the blessings God has for you, and it tries to rule you so that you won't experience the full force of Christ's love. Shame makes a difficult path even more treacherous and deadly.

But it doesn't have to be that way.

Shaking Off the Shackles of Shame

One of the greatest obstacles to enjoying the blessings God grants us is the heavy weight of shame. Sadly, many people don't understand the power of shame and what it's doing to them, the prison it keeps them in. Shame isolates us and weighs on us, burdening us with the past in ways that try to sabotage our glorious future. However, the good news is that through salvation in Jesus Christ, we have freedom from shame.

You see, everyone has a past. You're not on your own with shame over past mistakes and failures. Everyone has things they want to forget, things they want to leave behind, things that haunt them with sleepless nights. So often, we allow our past to define our frame of mind, the way we feel and the way we think.

Whether your past indiscretions were years ago or as recent as last night, there is power over the bondage that sin wraps around you. The Bible tells us that the wages of sin is death (see Rom. 6:23). If you think about that for a moment, you realize that what we earn when we sin is our own destruction. We usually think about earning wages for a paycheck, but when we sin we earn the wages of death.

Grace, on the other hand, grants us a gift—the precious gift of righteousness before God. We don't have to earn it—we couldn't if we tried—so we only have to ask for it and accept it. "For if by the one man's offense death reigned through the one, much more those who receive abundance of grace and of the gift of righteousness will reign in life through the One, Jesus Christ" (Rom. 5:17).

Are you ruling and reigning in life?

Are you living in dominion?

Consider what this verse says to us as followers of Jesus today: "The gift of righteousness will cause you to reign in life through Jesus Christ." You're called to flourish in life, to enjoy that wide-open, free, and abundant life we have through Christ. Here's how the Old Testament describes this gift: "The righteous shall flourish like a palm tree." It goes on, "He shall grow like a cedar in Lebanon. Those who are planted in the house of the LORD shall flourish in the courts of our God" (Ps. 92:12–13).

If you're living under the weight of guilt, of shame, of condemnation, you're not flourishing. You're not ruling and reigning.
Scripture tells us the righteous can reign in life. You can rule and
have dominion, but if you're living in shame, you're not ruling,
but instead being ruled. Instead of having dominion, you're being
dominated—dominated by things that have no power or value
in your life whatsoever.

You can live thinking that you owe it to yourself to feel bad
about things that have gone on before. And I'm not saying you
should ever take your past sins lightly. What I am saying is that
there's real hope in Jesus. Your focus should be on following
Christ, not on looking over your shoulder and regretting what you
can't change. Shame is a prison, but the door to your cell is open.

Jesus calls you to follow him in the freedom of grace.

Wise Up

One of my favorite verses is from Proverbs 15:24: "The way of life
winds upward for the wise." Sadly, rather than winding upward,
some people go on a steep decline, a downward spiral, because
here's what happens: Sin leads to guilt, guilt leads to shame, and
ultimately shame leads to condemnation. Condemnation leads
to death.

If a building is condemned, that means it's unfit for use. It's
disqualified. It's only good for being pulled down. That's how a
lot of people live their lives. They live feeling condemned, unfit
when it comes to serving God, perhaps even when it comes to
being in the house of God, when it comes to worship, when it
comes to the grace of God. They feel unworthy, unforgivable,
and even unlovable.

Some people are saved but they're not free. They don't believe they deserve to be happy, to enjoy the spacious, joyful life God has for them. They feel as if they're disqualified. They're unfit for happiness. But it's not true! It's nothing more than the devil's lies.

Sin becomes guilt, which is something we feel, an emotion. However, shame is something you carry, a state of being. People will sometimes say, "Shame on you!" and try to throw it at you. They judge you, condemn you, and try to make you feel the harsh sting of their rejection.

Have you ever had shame put on you? Ever feel worse because of the way others treated you or looked at you after they knew what you had done? While sin is something we do, and emotions are something we feel, shame is on a different level. It's something you carry, a weight and a burden. You walk down the street with it and feel it pressing down on you. Ultimately, it's exactly the opposite of the blessing of God.

If we want to shake off shame, we must understand the full power of what Jesus Christ has done for us. If you carry shame, then you're not carrying what comes with the blessing of God. With the blessing of God, you have the full benefit of all that's in his name. There is no other name that provides salvation that liberates the captives, that forgives the condemnation of sin. If you allow other things to be put on you, if you allow other things to rob you and rule you and bind you, then unfortunately you're living far short of what God has got for you.

Sin belittles you. The Bible tells us, "For all have sinned and fall short of the glory of God" (Rom. 3:23). If you think about that, if you fall short of the glory of God, it means that sin makes you smaller. It diminishes you—your potential, your relationship with God, and your confidence. You can't walk around with boldness and confidence if you're walking around hanging your head with the heavy weight of shame.

When people live ruled by shame, it has a huge toxic effect. They live under the power of condemnation, like someone with a black cloud constantly hanging over them. In fact, *The Message* often describes condemnation as a black cloud, one that's always about to send a thunderbolt to punish you.

But this does not align with the truth of God's Word and the power of Christ's death and resurrection. We're told, "God so loved the world that He gave His only Begotten Son" (John 3:16). And we're also told exactly why he sent him: "God did not send His Son into the world to condemn the world, but that the world through Him might be saved" (John 3:17). So many people know well the first part of this verse, but the fullness of its power is actually revealed in the second. Your Father wanted to give you the freedom of a full and vibrant life; he wanted you to experience salvation and life in abundance.

So he sent Jesus.

Orange Juice Never Tasted So Good

We've got to learn how to live our lives as saved men and women. And that means freedom from sin, freedom from guilt, freedom from shame, freedom from condemnation. Remember, sin is something you do, guilt is something you feel, and shame is something you carry. And eventually the weight of shame overtakes you and then condemnation takes you out. Condemnation would have you believe that just like a condemned building, you too are unfit for use.

That's not the will of God for you at all. And we never reach a point where we don't need reminding. When our path becomes difficult, shame will attempt to hijack our route. Sometimes it's when life is going well and you're enjoying a major blessing from the Lord. The devil can't stand for you to enjoy God's goodness without trying to thwart you and smother you with shame.

I know firsthand the way shame can ambush you from around the next corner.

Back in 2002, Hillsong Church had just completed a major building expansion and dedicated our new worship and convention center. At that time we were known around the world because of our worship music, but in Australia most people had never heard of us. The average person on the street probably didn't know we existed.

However, we suddenly burst through the surface of mainstream culture in an unforgettable way. Like many countries, Australia's largest newspapers have their big editions on weekends, usually with a splashy magazine in the center of the paper. So one Saturday not long after our new facility had been completed, the newspaper with Australia's largest circulation came out with Bobbie and me on the cover of their weekend magazine. Nothing about it was flattering.

We were so humiliated and upset, so hurt. We had naively cooperated and posed for photos with the writer of the article several weeks earlier and had tried to be as transparent as possible. And now it had bitten us. We felt blindsided and deceived, duped into believing it would be a fair and balanced portrait of us and our ministry. But it wasn't. The article was several pages long and a total misrepresentation, completely twisting our motives and belittling everything we stood for.

I remember feeling so ashamed. So embarrassed. We were in Bondi Beach the same Saturday morning that the papers hit. It was the weekend, so everyone was out and about, enjoying the beach and the beautiful weather. Cafés were crowded with throngs of people relaxing and enjoying a leisurely breakfast alfresco. And it seemed like everyone was reading the paper, holding up the weekend magazine with our picture and its terrible caption.

I remember walking along the familiar boardwalk, a place we loved and where we previously felt at home, but now feeling so humiliated, so embarrassed. Eventually that morning, we went into a café ourselves to have breakfast. We had been there lots of times, so we were familiar to the staff. I was feeling embarrassed and trying to keep my head down low so that no one would recognize me when our waiter came and I ordered an orange juice. A couple minutes later he returned with the most amazing glass of OJ I've ever seen. Instead of just the normal juice glass, my drink had all these beautiful fruit garnishes all around the rim of this giant tumbler of fresh-squeezed orange juice. After setting it before me, our waiter looked at me and said, "You're a good guy."

His words, his kindness, and the unspoken reference he was making spoke to my soul. They broke the yoke of shame bearing down on me. I've never felt so grateful to a waiter in a restaurant before. It's amazing how God uses moments in our lives to communicate and assure us of his love. He wanted me to know that just because the paper had printed all these distortions and fabrications didn't mean that everyone believed it.

I've been back to Bondi many times since that bittersweet Saturday morning. The beach there is one of my favorite places in the world. I refused to allow shame to rule me then, and I forbid shame from clinging to me now. I've also learned not to be ruled by the opinions and attitudes of others. I'm a free man because of the grace of Jesus Christ. I am loved by my Heavenly Father beyond measure.

And so are you.

Flourish in Freedom

You have to understand the victory that God gives you over shame. I believe you've got to learn how to walk tall in the good news of the gospel of our Lord, Jesus Christ. He gives you every reason to hold your head up and walk tall and refuse to allow shame to be put on you. Live free.

We don't have to throw off the shame that tries to lock us in a choke hold on our own. Christ has broken its power for us. "There is therefore now no condemnation to those who are in Christ Jesus, who do not walk according to the flesh, but according to the Spirit" (Rom. 8:1). Notice the distinction this verse makes. It doesn't say you won't have temptation, and it doesn't say that things won't try to rear their ugly heads at times. But there is no condemnation! It has no claim on you and your big, abundant life of freedom in Christ. God wants to break the power of shame over your life.

What about you? Can you believe that you have absolutely nothing to be ashamed of because of what Jesus has done for you? Or are you still condemning yourself? Maybe you believe that God has forgiven you. Maybe you accept that other people are willing to forgive you for the ways you've hurt them. But are you willing to let God's grace sink down into your bones?

The path of life has enough difficulties of its own without us making it harder than it has to be. Don't allow the enemy to taunt you with your past mistakes. God doesn't remember them, so why should you? Righteousness is your free gift. Live in it, soak it up, and flourish like a palm tree.

You live by faith, not by shame.

You are loved.
You are free.
You are forgiven.
Shame has no claim on you.
You belong to Jesus.

CHAPTER NINE

Lean on Me

I believe in God, Our Father,
I believe in Christ the Son.
I believe in the Holy Spirit, Our God is three in One.
I believe in the resurrection, that we will rise again.
For I believe in the Name of Jesus.
"This I Believe (The Creed)," Hillsong Music, 2014

My pulpit is bigger than yours."

These words, said with a smirk by an Australian journalist to me, framed twelve years of intense scrutiny by the media. In fact, we have a storeroom in our church office with shelves that are entirely dedicated to years' worth of newspaper clippings, videotapes, CDs, and DVDs filled with stories about Hillsong Church in the Australian media.

For the most part, it wasn't only what the media said about Bobbie and me and Hillsong Church—it was what they ignored that was the most hurtful. Responses were rarely published, and people with antireligious agendas seemed to drive much of the negative perception that framed what our community believed about us.

Some of it I brought upon myself. In the early days of Hillsong

Church, I wrote a book titled *You Need More Money*. What was I thinking? I was young and eager, with little influence outside of our own local church, and I thought readers would be drawn to a provocative title. I may as well have painted a bull's-eye on my head, because critics took the title and labeled us "prosperity preachers" teaching a "prosperity gospel." I hate that term! There has only ever been one gospel, and one gospel alone—the gospel of Jesus Christ.

Perhaps the criticism of this book could best be summed up in a conversation that a friend of mine had with an evangelical pastor who joined in the chorus of opinions. Directly after his damning assessment of the book (which he later admitted he had never actually read), he shared with my friend how desperate their church was for a youth pastor, but they lacked the necessary funds to hire one. And therein lies the thesis of my book!

You see, without money, it's hard (as a ministry, a business, a family) to fulfill the kingdom endeavors that are in your heart. Missionaries need money, churches need money, educating your children requires money. In fact, the book itself outlines many of the perils that come with the love of money and how God is not interested in attitudes of greed, but it also says he cares about blessing us so that, in turn, we might use what we have to equip us and others for the journey. Or, as God put it to Abraham, "I will bless you and make your name great; and you shall be a blessing" (Gen. 12:2).

In reality, I should have taken far more care so that the book couldn't have been taken out of context and lost its effectiveness. It is an unwise person who doesn't learn a lesson from such criticism. Even if facts were wrong or skewed, perceptions can teach us things and cause us to be better and do better—if we let them.

The amazing thing about all this criticism was that through every season of it, the support Bobbie and our children and I personally received from our own local church and from many others was unparalleled. All these attempts to discourage us and throw mud at us only caused people who knew differently through their own experience of Hillsong to rise up in courage and stand firm on what they believed—that Bobbie and I have always endeavored to live by the principles that we teach others.

One of the things I learned through these trials was just how resilient God's Church is. God says, "I will build my church, and the gates of Hades shall not prevail against it" (Matt. 16:18), and we saw this to be true in every way—as we grew not only in size but in influence. What I also learned is that it's not what the media says that will hurt you; it's what the media says that is *true*. Therefore practicing what we preach and doing the journey in front of our church family and community with openness and transparency is paramount.

Developing the courage to live with conviction and accountability is the doorway to fulfillment in life, love, and leadership. In my experience, it is always worth the effort to work through hurt and disappointment, and see your less-than-ideal circumstances as opportunity for growth and learning, rather than becoming a victim. There are three ways to learn from our mistakes: the easy way, the hard way, and the tragic way. The easy way is learning from other people's mistakes. The hard way is learning from our own. And the tragic way is not learning from either.

Don't waste your mistakes by not learning from them—allow them to teach you, allow yourself to grow in them and become a better person because of them. And when your worst day becomes a long season, you can take courage from knowing that there will be faithful people who are ready and willing to make the journey alongside you every bumpy step of the way.

Live Transparently

One of the great temptations, when life's path becomes difficult, is to isolate yourself. It is a natural instinct to try to pull back from your emotions and not feel the sharp pain caused by your crisis. If you're like me in such moments, you may also feel the need to retreat and become isolated. Even when you're around people, you can withdraw emotionally. Going through a trial, a temptation, or turmoil makes you feel quite vulnerable, so it's natural to want to put up your walls and hide behind them. But that never helps the problem and it's little comfort. When you least feel like having fellowship with others is often when you need it the most. God understands the value of relationship, the value of the team. By nature, he exists as a trinity—a concept I just love. He is the God of the universe, and yet he still chooses to partner with us to see his plans and purposes worked out on the earth.

God's Word certainly bears out this truth: "And let us consider how we may spur one another on toward love and good deeds, not giving up meeting together, as some are in the habit of doing, but encouraging one another—and all the more as you see the Day approaching" (Heb. 10:24–25 NIV). When you're struggling through a difficult part of your path, the best thing you can do is get into a great, positive, faith-filled environment.

And this is where the local church can be so invaluable.

Bobbie and I always aspired to build a church that was youthful in spirit, generous at heart, faith filled in confession, loving in nature, and inclusive in expression. Sadly, I recognize that not every community has a healthy expression of the local church, and this is where we need to be planted in the Word of God— so we can speak to our own soul, claim victory, and rise up in Jesus' name. But remember, the perfect church doesn't exist, so don't underestimate the value of building healthy, God-glorifying relationships wherever your find yourself.

As we discussed in earlier chapters, David understood the process of pain. But he also realized the incredible importance of allowing others to support him. After his prayer that God would release his soul from prison (Psalm 142), he declared, "the righteous shall surround me" (v. 7).

David knew that when you're feeling surrounded by accusation or by people who don't understand you or care about your suffering, that's when you need God's people the most. I encourage you to choose, during times of difficulty and discouragement and despite your natural inclination, to plant yourself in an environment where praise can take your focus off your problems and restore your gaze on an eternal perspective. Do all you can to get around people who can sit with you in your pain and not try to fix your problems or give you pat answers. People who will carry you with their faith when yours feels a bit weak and beaten up.

In the same way, it is unwise to trust your heart's pain with just anyone. You've got to gather trusted confidants, people you love and trust, people who know your heart and can handle your fragile state. The Bible tells us, "Where there is no counsel, the people fall; but in the multitude of counselors there is safety" (Prov. 11:14). Notice it says a multitude of *counselors*, not a multitude of opinions. So don't trust just anyone—the neighbor on the corner, the lady in the checkout line, the guy at the gym, or the coworker at the office. Instead, focus on the people who share your faith.

It has amazed me in the past to see people lose their way when they allow their hairdresser, whose own world is a catastrophe, to become their counselor. Nothing against hairdressers, but the same can be said of unchurched colleagues and neighbors. Sharing your woes with people whose own lives don't line up with the will of God can lead to bad advice and poor choices. Look for the people in your life who love you and love God and clearly want what's best for you, with no agendas or strings attached.

Sympathy or Compassion?

Everyone loves a little sympathy.

In the Old Testament, one of the kings of Israel, King Ahab, sought counsel from four hundred prophets before he went into battle. All four hundred prophets were sympathetic to their ruler, and they told the king what he wanted to hear: that yes, the Lord would surely bring him victory. But there was one young prophet who chose to hear from the Lord, not bow to the power of intimidation. In 1 Kings 22 we see that even the king himself recognized that he was simply searching for people who would sympathize with him and bring a good word that justified what he wanted to do. After calling all four hundred prophets together, "the King of Israel replied to Jehoshaphat, 'There is one more man who could consult the LORD for us, but I hate him. He never prophesies anything but trouble for me!'" (v. 8 NLT).

This story always makes me smile—the king outwardly

confessing he would rather hear what he wants to hear, rather than the truth. Have you ever avoided someone because they were a truth teller and had things to say that you didn't want to hear? I have, and let me tell you, it certainly didn't help me then and it won't help you now.

When you're going through a rough patch, you want friends, colleagues, mentors, or pastors who have the guts to tell you the truth and to remind you of God's truth—not people who are simply trying to please you. People who will give you advice motivated by love and not judgment, condemnation, or manipulation.

My own experience has led me many times to receive counsel from people who are older than me or more mature in their faith and have come through their own challenges—people who have grown stronger from it and can offer you real support, wisdom, love, and assurance.

Not one time do we ever find Jesus being moved with sympathy; but every time he was moved with *compassion* something powerful was about to happen—a miracle was on its way. That's because sympathy identifies with the problem, but compassion gets up, looks up, and says, "I need to do something about this."

So when you are struggling on the difficult path, find someone who will look you in the eye, put their hands on your shoulders, and tell you the unvarnished truth, the truth of God's love, hope, healing, and power in your life.

Love Authentically

It is just as important to find people who will do the journey with you as it is to become a better person on the journey yourself. When you're going through a difficult stretch, you also have an opportunity to bless and help the people around you. You have the chance to bring your family, friends, and loved ones with you on your journey, to share in what God's doing in your life and show leadership as you authentically and honestly walk the difficult path.

When you're suffering and struggling, you have a spotlight on your life. When Bobbie and I have faced opposition from others, we know that as much as we hurt, our kids always felt our pain a whole lot more, and our church family would also be feeling the weight of scrutiny from neighbors, colleagues, and peers. Knowing we had a chance to exercise faith, especially in the midst of our pain, helped us to focus on God and not on our circumstances. We didn't want our kids to think we had stopped trusting in God's power and goodness just because we hit a rough patch. This was when they needed to see what we believed in action.

Disappointment and hurt is an opportunity to be transparent, but don't be pitiful—and there is a difference. This process can be challenging, compounded by the more people you have watching you. It is at times like these that our human nature is to put on a brave face for those around us, but to vent and even lash out at the people who are closest to us in the midst of heartache. Often spouses are "sacrificed" to our unredeemed emotions during times of anguish and pain—and yet the people closest to us are the ones we need the most. Don't forgo good relationships for a moment of hurt and anger—learn to lean firmly on those who have promised to remain faithful in the good times and bad.

Leadership, at any level, is so often proven in the tough times— there is definitely a strength in revealing yourself as human and vulnerable in these moments without collapsing in despair. By

God's grace, he has brought Hillsong through every trial that's ever arisen—continually winding upward rather than spiraling downward—but it hasn't come without a cost. As leaders, Bobbie and I always made the decision to never let the crisis create a bigger crisis. And we never let anything deter us from what God called us to do: love God and love people.

I'm convinced that when you let people know what's going on and where you are at, with transparency and authenticity, they respond positively and want to rally behind you.

This process of transparency does not mean getting defensive and blaming others. When I ride my motorcycle, which is not very often these days, I ride it with the attitude that any potential accident is my fault. Because it's a motorbike, you don't get too many second chances. So in other words, whether someone pulls out in front of me or cuts me off, I'm still the one taking the risk and facing a potential life-threatening accident. So I ride in a posture that makes me responsible for whatever happens to me on the highway. Obviously, I can't control other drivers and their choices and mistakes, but that's part of the risk I assume whenever I choose to ride.

I try to lead the same way, not by blaming others or assuming someone else is at fault but by taking responsibility for my decisions and whatever happens. You can always find reasons why you're not to blame and why you're the victim. But this is no way to lead your life, and it will ultimately undermine the big, spacious life you want to live as you follow Jesus.

Jesus faced unbelievable pressure many times in his ministry on earth—when news of Lazarus' grave illness reached him, when he was tempted in the wilderness by Satan, in Gethsemane, and on the cross—and yet every time he remained focused and unwavering in his Spirit. Satan will use pressure and opposition to try to control you and when we yield to pressure, we surrender our leadership. It is important to deal with circumstances when opposition arises, but don't allow it to control you.

Moving On

Many years ago we came up against one of the most bizarre and unforeseen challenges we have ever faced. Our church had just put out a new album, and literally within days we discovered that one of the songs on the album, which was attracting a lot of attention, had been written by someone who was not only living a lie, but had knowingly deceived many people with a fabricated story that evoked people's attention and compassion.

Not wanting to perpetuate this person's deception, we had a difficult decision to make. The immediate impact of these revelations included a huge financial burden and involved recalling thousands of DVDs. The ongoing impact of this deceptive behavior could very well have devastated many lives and the consequences could have been catastrophic both locally within our own church and globally in the Christian community.

However, it was at that time that even though I felt completely duped and disappointed, I had to lead the church in a way that encouraged people who were hurt and confused to rise above the disappointment and find God in the midst of their questions. I called on others to choose to see this person from the perspective of his human frailties and extend forgiveness rather than take offense. In these moments we can choose to allow disappointment to create a root of bitterness or deep-seated hurt in us, or we can allow it to humble us and extend understanding and love. Such disappointment is an opportunity to evaluate and consider our own lives and the effect we can have on those around us.

Incredibly, the issue itself was very short-lived within our church. In leadership generally, I have learned that if it is a problem to me, it will be a problem to those around me. And therefore it is important to not pretend everything is okay but simply address the issue, shift focus, and move on.

Lead Courageously

Finally, as you walk the difficult path with others—as you lean into their strength—stay focused on forward motion. Learn from the past, yes, especially if there are choices you could have made differently—that's Wisdom 101. But you must also embrace the present and realize that you can't change the past. You must move forward with courage, not rushing things, but not staying fixated on whatever trauma has occurred.

One of the best ways to move forward according to God's timing is to focus on his goodness. We're told, "Whatever things are true, whatever things are noble, whatever things are just, whatever things are pure, whatever things are lovely, whatever things are of good report, if there is any virtue and if there is anything praiseworthy—meditate on these things" (Phil. 4:8). When we beat ourselves up over what might have happened or what might have been, we miss out on what God wants to give us moving forward and what he wants to teach us in the present.

When we're struggling along in pain, it's tempting to follow the exact opposite of this exhortation. When speaking to our congregation I lightheartedly like to make a point clear by highlighting the way our human nature often thinks, with what I like to call my "Opposite World Translation." In this instance it goes something like this: "Whatever things are rumor or hearsay, whatever things are negative, whatever things are mean, whatever things are trashy, whatever things dig up the dirt, whatever things bring a juicy report, if there are any skeletons in the closet, anything gossip worthy, think on these things."

Are you living according to the Opposite World Translation, or are you living according to the Word of God? Because it's good to focus on the positive report when you are surrounded completely by the negative data. Don't say you're focused on God's point of view when you're really looking over your shoulder or at your feet. Look ahead! Look up! And travel on your journey of faith with people who will reset your spiritual compass if it goes astray. Live through crisis with courage and an authority that points people to the One with answers, not the one with problems.

And never forget, ultimately God will bring you through your current trial. He will deliver you from present circumstances and redeem your suffering. And one of the best ways he accomplishes both results is through his people. So when the path grows dim and you feel like giving up, turn to your brothers and sisters, your fellow believers, your local church, and lean on their strength. Let them in to your pain and allow them to share just a little of what you're going through. This is how we get through the hard parts of life. This is how we grow and this is how we lead.

Live transparently.

Love authentically.

And lead courageously.

CHAPTER TEN

The Original Pioneer

Open our eyes, to see the things that make Your
   heart cry,
to be the Church that You would desire, Your light
   to be seen.
      "With Everything," Hillsong Music, 2008

Imagine losing your brother to an incurable condition.

Then imagine discovering the ability to cure the incurable condition.

That is exactly what Christian Barnard, a cardiothoracic surgeon from Cape Town, did. He was the first surgeon to ever perform a human-to-human heart transplant in 1967. Years of research from fellow doctors and various experimental surgeries gave him the opportunity to pioneer this lifesaving medical procedure that has undoubtedly changed the face of modern medicine. Many would consider him the original heart pioneer, but there was another one even before him.

The Original Heart Pioneer

Of course, God himself is the original pioneer, creating the heavens and the earth out of the void. He created the first man and woman, something never attempted or accomplished before he breathed his life into dust to form flesh and blood. Through the generations that followed, pioneering seems to be in our DNA, which makes sense considering we're made in God's image.

John 1:1 says, "In the beginning was the Word, and the Word was with God, and the Word was God." Verse 14 goes on to say, "And the Word became flesh and dwelt among us." There's no mistaking it: From the very beginning, God pioneered! Similarly, Hebrews 4:12 says, "For the Word of God is living and powerful, and sharper than any two-edged sword, piercing even to the division of soul and spirit, and of joints and marrow, and is a discerner of the thoughts and intents of the heart."

I love the way the Bible describes the Word of God as being not only powerful, but sharper than a two-edged sword—so sharp that it can divide between not only soul and spirit but between joints and marrow. Now that's precision! The Bible, the Word of God, has the ability—with even greater precision than Dr. Christian Barnard—to divide between the thoughts and intents of the heart.

Jesus pioneers internally and outworks externally. The Bible describes him as the pioneer of our salvation, the pioneer of our faith. And I would describe him as the pioneer of our hearts. Salvation is something that Christ does in our heart that changes our eternal destiny. It changes your reason for being, it changes your sense of purpose, it changes the way you live, it changes the reason for our gifts and talents, it changes our families and our marriages. Ultimately salvation that starts in the heart has an impact on generations to come.

What is it that is in your heart?

Pioneer *and* Perfector

The story has been told that after Walt Disney passed away, his wife, Lilly, was at the opening of the newest theme park, Walt Disney World in Orlando, Florida. During the ceremony, one of her friends leaned over and said, "Shame Walt isn't here to see this." To which Lilly replied, "Walt did see this—that's why it's here."

What do you presently see when you close your eyes? What vision or dream has God planted in your heart for you to nurture and cultivate? What vision sustains you when you're hurting and afraid, shocked and stunned by life's events?

God is indeed a great pioneer, and I believe that he not only gives you visions and dreams, but he always completes what he begins. God doesn't start something in us so that we can live frustrated, restrained, bitter lives. Jesus is called the Author and Finisher of our faith, or as another translation renders it, the Pioneer and the Perfector. God has planted something in you that he intends to bring to fruition if you will just keep your dream and your vision alive. He wants us thriving in the wide-open territory where our souls can flourish! This is particularly important to remember on the difficult path.

It's your heart that plans your way and determines your ability to experience the big life God has in store for you. In Scripture, we see the apostle John greeting his friend, "Beloved, I pray that you may prosper in all things and be in health, just as your soul prospers" (3 John 1:2).

This ability to prosper is not just about material blessings so much as it's about an internal state of peace, joy, and fulfillment in how you live your life. In fact, I believe that when we thrive internally, then blessing can ultimately outwork itself in every area of life. It starts on the inside, in our heart.

When the path gets difficult, we often have to stop and regroup, to pause and check our directions. But the internal compass attuned to God's spirit is our heart. The Psalmist says, "My heart is overflowing with a good theme; I recite my composition concerning the King; My tongue is the pen of a ready writer" (Ps. 45:1). Every story is written to a good theme—and the theme of your heart determines the story of your life.

David says, "My heart also instructs me in the night seasons" (Ps. 16:7). So many things breed in the night. Fear and anxiety breed in the night. Confusion and discouragement, desperation and discontent breed in the night. How many people do you know who have lost their way in the pitch-black of the night season? Yet as we read in the Bible, the theme of David's heart enabled him to say, "The lines have fallen to me in pleasant places; yes, I have a good inheritance. I will bless the LORD who has given me counsel...I have set the LORD always before me" (Ps. 16:6–7, 8).

When trials come and obstacles pop up on life's path, the way you recalibrate and renew your journey is by keeping your heart focused on God. How you live your life tends to reflect the overflow of your heart. If you lose the vision, the dream that God has planted in you, then you will ultimately lose your way.

A Captain in the Storm

Bobbie and I had only been married a couple of days when we encountered rough waters. And I mean that literally! We didn't have much money so we were enjoying a budget-style honeymoon, staying in little motels and camping cabins around our native New Zealand. Nothing fancy, but we were young, happy, and passionately in love.

I had borrowed my mum's car to drive around the South Island before we woke up early to catch the big interisland ferry between the North and South Islands. These ships are not like the little ferryboats that zip tourists and workers between Sydney Harbour and its famous Manly Beach. These ferries were enormous carriers, large enough for hundreds of cars in the hull, freight trains, and even more passengers on deck.

Sitting in the front lounge, along with dozens of others, we faced huge windows opening onto the bow of the ship. We were up about three stories high, and the view was spectacular. I remember an older man and his young grandson standing by the floor-to-ceiling windows and chatting excitedly before the crew asked us all to be seated.

Our ship turned out of the harbor and into a stretch of water notorious for being rough. In fact, only a few years earlier, a huge passenger ferry sailing between Lyttelton and Wellington had capsized during a storm of historic proportions. While the ship, the *Wahine*, was only a few hundred meters from shore, in the heads of the Wellington Harbour, many people perished because the ocean was so rough; the current pulled them into open seas and rescuers could not get to them.

The day was a bit overcast—not unusual, though, along the

coast where the morning sun later burned the clouds away. However, as we left the harbor behind us, the dark clouds intensified and the wind picked up dramatically. At first it felt as if we were on a roller coaster, riding the waves up and down as they rocked us. Soon it was clear that this was not going to be easy as the waves grew higher and higher, and we pitched sharply. As the angry dark green waves increased in size and intensity, they began coming over the rails of the decks below us. We watched as walls of water formed around us—yes, *walls* of water!

The bow of the ship continued taking the full force of the fierce oncoming waves. But then suddenly, almost as if in slow motion, a giant wave came from the side. The bow dipped beneath the water, pummeled by the wave's sheer force, and we watched in terror as the wave came up over the decks below us and crashed into the windows of the lounge. Out of natural instinct, we closed our eyes and braced ourselves in our chairs as the wave crashed through the windows and in on us.

After several seconds, Bobbie and I opened our eyes in shock. People began screaming, soaked and bleeding from the broken glass everywhere. The sharp, salty smell of the ocean assaulted us as water flooded into the interior of the ship. Later, I read in the newspaper about one poor man who had been in the bathroom in the back of the lounge. He had been using the toilet when he looked up and saw a wave of water coming over the cubicle door! Can you imagine? One minute you're using the loo and the next thing you know it's like a water park ride. I guess it was a good thing he was sitting down!

I took Bobbie by the hand and we proceeded through knee-deep water toward the back of the ship. Crew members dashed about madly trying to sort through the chaos. Glass, blood, and floating objects like hats and purses littered the aisles. I remember feeling as if I needed to assure my new bride that everything would be okay, so I said something like "Don't worry, Bobbie, we'll be all right—and if we're not, then we'll be in heaven! It's just a matter of how we get there!" Not exactly the most comforting words, but she knew my heart.

Our captain, familiar with these waters, stopped the boat and let it list until it was safe to make headway again. He knew we had to deal with the aftermath: bail out the water and restore our course settings before we could continue. I'm not sure I would have had the calm demeanor to focus on what needed to be done to bring the ship to seaworthy status. But thank God for a captain who was calm in his heart, who not only knew the course and could see the shore, but had prepared for the journey.

Many were the secrets and dreams in our young hearts—I am grateful to God that our captain never lost his vision! Needless to say, our journey into the glorious unknown of our future together started with turbulent waters—but oh, what a ride!

Secrets of the Heart

What's overflowing in your heart right now? What is the composition, the story, your life is telling? Is your tongue willing to declare your trust in God during life's storms? Or is your tongue complaining, grumbling, and despairing when the waves crash in?

If you want to experience a long, joyful life, then you must hold tight to the vision God placed inside you—strive less and envision more. If there's a secret to living the big, wide-open, abundant life, then it all comes back to what's going on inside your heart. God plants such beautiful things in our hearts. We often think of secrets in a negative way, and certainly many secrets can be painful, if not harmful. So often we think of secrets as skeletons in the cupboard—things we don't want people to find out. But what about those "secrets" that God has pioneered in your heart, something that's just between the two of you—a desire, a yearning, a longing, something that brings tears to your eyes and stirs something deep down inside you.

Not long ago, I encouraged my congregation to write down the visions of their hearts. What is the one thing that God has spoken to you about that you are perhaps too afraid to say out loud? If you could dream a big dream, one that nobody would laugh or scoff at…what would it be? It amazed me how many people told me they were afraid to do it!

There could be so many wonderful things, maybe so many personal things in your heart that God has birthed there. Perhaps the dreams are so tender, so vulnerable, and so personal that you've never told anybody. Maybe you've just told your spouse about some deep longing, some deep belief, some incredible dream that God put in your heart. Well, I can tell you with absolutely certainty that what he's put in your heart—he wants to be complete in your life.

In Luke 2 is a passage about Mary, the mother of Jesus. It was twelve years on from when an angel spoke to Mary and told her she would conceive, that she pondered these things in her heart. Later, we are told that Jesus, as a twelve-year-old was found in the temple, "he went down to Nazareth with them and was obedient to them. But his mother treasured all these things in her heart" (v. 51 NIV). Mary reacted to the mystery of her son in the temple in the same way that she reacted to the news of her virgin conception. She kept these secrets in her heart. As a human being, Mary undoubtedly struggled to understand the divine plan in which she consented to participate; however, her grace and obedience to God and his vision for her life meant that she continued to outwork the things she held secret and sacred.

What's kept in your heart? What do you need to guard in your heart because you don't want to fall short of everything God intends for you? I have often found that when your path is blocked and life has forced you to stop and recalculate your route, God's secret in your heart can help you keep going.

Hannah is another woman in the Bible who knew about secrets of the heart. She had a burning desire to have a child, even though it seemed physically impossible. Married to a man named Elkanah, Hannah struggled with anger in her soul and a sharp, jagged pain in her heart over her situation. But notice that she refuses to give up her hope, the vision of birthing a baby boy that God had planted in her heart:

> And she was in bitterness of soul, and prayed to the LORD and wept in anguish. Then she made a vow and said, "O LORD of hosts, if You will indeed look on the affliction of Your maidservant and remember me, and not forget Your maidservant, but will give Your maidservant a male child, then I will give him to the LORD all the days of his life, and no razor shall come upon his head."
>
> And it happened, as she continued praying before the LORD, that Eli watched her mouth. Now Hannah *spoke in her heart*; only her lips moved, but her voice was not heard. (1 Samuel 1:10–13; emphasis added)

Isn't that a fascinating way to phrase Hannah's petition before God? "Now Hannah spoke in her heart." I wonder exactly how that works, although all of us, myself included, can understand this inner voice, this inner burning desire. Hannah spoke in her heart, and only her lips moved without any sound coming from her mouth. Eli, the temple priest, assumed she was either a crazy woman or drunk!

When have you felt like Hannah in your desperate desire to hold to the vision God has given you? Sometimes when you can't verbalize all that God has placed in your heart, you struggle to give voice to it. You can't articulate it, and worry that if you try it would only sound silly or stupid. Maybe those who heard it wouldn't understand and instead would think you were bragging or even delusional. But what God places in our hearts is so precious and beautiful, we must hold those secrets closely and guard them.

Years ago and still today, when I close my eyes I see an outpost of grace, a church so large the city could not ignore it—a healthy, functional, and glorious Body of Christ. Long before there were a few dozen people meeting in a schoolroom in a suburb of Sydney, long before there was a Hillsong Church in Australia, let alone one in more than a dozen other countries, I saw this vision in my heart. Now we've seen God do so many amazing things, it exceeds anything I could've imagined. Nonetheless, I've held on to that church that we pioneered inside my heart ever since I was a young man. Were there times when I thought we might never make it? Of course! But I never lost sight of the vision in my heart.

Notice also how Hannah's longing took time to come to life. "So it came to pass in the process of time that Hannah conceived and bore a son, and called his name Samuel, saying, 'Because I have asked for him from the LORD'" (1 Sam. 1:20). Maybe it's going to take some time, maybe even several seasons of your life, for what's been conceived in your heart to come to life. So many dreams take time: health restored, marriages healed, businesses started, children saved, families reunited, relationships mended.

If what the Lord has deposited in your heart has not produced fruit, don't give up. Just keep the hope alive in your heart and guard it. Close your eyes and make sure your vision remains clear so that even if circumstances seem to thwart your dream at every turn, you can keep it alive until God's time for it to be born.

Pour Out Your Heart

Years ago, my mum told me a story of a time I would have been too young to remember. My father, who had been a Salvation Army officer, was unemployed, and not only that, he was unemployable—due to two recent nervous breakdowns. My mum was raising five children in one room, was penniless, and had a husband who had lost all perspective and vision and had no means of support. One day, when she was hanging out the clothes in the backyard in New Zealand, she literally flung herself in despair over the clothesline and cried out to God, "I can't take this anymore!"

Well, God met her in that place. She recalls slumping over with a sigh—desperate for answers from the Lord. What does that sigh represent to you? What is it in your life that you currently don't understand, feel in despair about, or can't come to terms with? Because the very same pioneer who authored your salvation can also renew faith in your heart—and the power of faith in your heart can lead to a breakthrough in your life.

What's your longing? That tender, vulnerable thing that you can't even give words to? In Psalm 62:8 the Psalmist says, "Trust in him at all times, you people; pour out your hearts to him" (NIV).

Pour out your heart to him, for God is our refuge.

Weathering the Storm

Sometimes we have no choice but to hang on and let life's "waves"—unpredictable circumstances like sickness and death, financial hardship, and unexpected loss—crash over us. But then we have to be like the captain of the ferry Bobbie and I were on. We have to assess the damage, remediate and resolve as much as we can, and then refocus our attention and energies on where we're headed. We have to make sure our heart's setting is on what God wants for us, what he has instilled in us, and what he wants to develop in our lives.

As you consider taking the next step and then the next when the path gets difficult, you often discover that you must pause and reset your course. When life gets hard and the waves are crashing around you, you can't stick your head in the sand and pretend otherwise. But you also can't allow the storms of life to capsize your journey permanently. It can be tempting to just stop and make excuses and then keep stalling instead of starting up again.

This temptation to get stuck in fear and self-pity reinforces why we must pause only long enough to restore our proper vision. Many times, the external obstacles in our path are not as heavy as the internal ones. When we're struggling with life's challenges, the greatest limitation we face may come from the issues of our heart. If we're not guarding and protecting what God has placed within our hearts, then we lose our vision and find it difficult to persevere. The vision you have for your life must be protected in your heart. When you encounter a difficult path, you must keep your eyes on the prize.

Keeping Hope Alive

December 27, 2012—I remember the day well, because Bobbie and I were flying out that day from Sydney to the United States, and before we went to the airport, we met with Joel and Esther (my eldest son and his new wife) for breakfast at Bondi Beach, in a little café called Trios. Ironically, they were in Sydney visiting from New York City, and we were on our way to New York City—such are our lives. I'll never forget that day because it was the day they told us they were pregnant.

We adore Esther and really felt like we had only just gotten over the shock and delight that our eldest son had finally got married—this baby news was pretty exciting! After our excited chatter and all the questions and congratulations, we went to pay for our breakfast, only to find that someone had already taken care of the bill! I always knew that whoever paid the bill that day would have heard our whole conversation—they would have heard Joel and Esther tell us they were pregnant, seen our rejoicing, and, I assume, felt happy for us. I always wondered who it was.

Well, one year later to that very day—December 27, 2013—I was going for a jog around the coastline. To be honest my jog was probably a little more like a fast walk, but as I was exercising a young guy reached his hand out on the path and said, "Excuse me, excuse me, Pastor Brian, can I talk to you, can I tell you a quick story?" And you know what it's like when you're exercising and someone wants you to stop, but he called me "Pastor Brian," so I thought I'd better stop. I quit jogging and this young guy walked alongside me as he began to tell me this story:

"Twelve months ago my wife and I were in a little café in Bondi having breakfast. We were desperate. We were desperate because we couldn't have children and we were hoping and believing that against all odds we were going to have a baby in the New Year. It was there in that café that we decided we were going to fast for the first thirty days of the New Year, and we had just made that decision when both you and Bobbie, Joel and Esther walked in and sat at the table almost right next to us."

He went on to tell me that he overheard Joel and Esther share with us their great news, and he admitted that in all honesty, it kind of hurt. There they were as a couple talking about their desperation and the longing of their hearts, only to overhear and witness someone else's joy. He said that despite the hurt they felt, they paid our bill anyway. I had spent twelve months wondering who paid that bill.

He went on to say, "We did what we said we were going to do, and we fasted for thirty days." The best part of the story is this: As he was telling me all of this he was jubilant, because he had a beautiful little two-month-old daughter strapped to a carrier on his chest. My eyes got moist as he shared with me their determination to hold on to the dreams in their heart and God's faithfulness in their desperation. I probably ran twice as fast to get back and tell Bobbie this incredible story. Praise God! He pioneered something in their hearts—and what he pioneered in their hearts, he completed in their lives.

Never Stop Pioneering

The same is true for you and the new territories God has for you. Just like Hannah and Mary, and like my friends on Bondi Beach, through keeping hope alive, keeping your vision alive, and protecting your heart, you keep fruitfulness alive in your life. Yes, the path will grow difficult, and the inevitable storms of life may crash through your windows and leave you drenched. But if you return to the secret God has placed in your heart, if you keep his vision alive for your future, then you will know the kind of contentment Paul described here: "I have learned in whatever state I am, to be content: I know how to be abased, and I know how to abound. Everywhere and in all things I have learned both to be full and to be hungry, both to abound and to suffer need. I can do all things through Christ who strengthens me" (Phil. 4:11–13).

PART 3

A Narrow Gate

CHAPTER ELEVEN

No Other Name

One Name holds weight above them all.
His fame outlasts the earth He formed.

"No Other Name," Hillsong Music, 2014

History's bowels have coughed up multitudes of names
chained to fame.
The tenacious, the notorious; the religious and
sacrilegious.
What images flit across the window of your mind
when you hear names such as Socrates and
Churchill, Mussolini, Mandela and Einstein?
Do you recoil when you hear Hitler?
Does inspiration hit you between the eyes when you
hear Armstrong?
Do you yawn and roll those same eyes when you think
of Shakespeare?
Names are pregnant with purpose. That's "what's in a
name."
And friends if I may inquire, what stirs within the
recesses of your soul when you hear Jesus' name?
An enigma personified, wholly man, wholly divine.
Took on the lowest names, so slaves could reign as kings.
Deity who chose to endure mortality, so we could
enjoy eternity.

Why does NO OTHER NAME affect the skeptic, the
   heretic and the majestic?
The homicidal, suicidal and the matinee idol?
NO OTHER NAME changed nature, mind-sets and
   matter.
Opened blind eyes, deaf ears and healed cancer.
NO OTHER NAME came with this mandate:
Heaven's Kingdom expressed on Earth.
But if His miracles are just "fairy tales,"
then why do millions gather putting their lives on the
   line for HIS name?
I've come to the conclusion that there is NO OTHER
   NAME!

   Lyrics by wordsmith Iseme Adeola (aka Isi the Scribe)

I love this passage. Our creative team penned and conceptualized these words, framing our live worship album and Hillsong Conference around these very thoughts and images. After the song "No Other Name" was written by my son Joel and Jonas Myrin, we (as a church) began to camp around the name of Jesus and the all-encompassing power, majesty, beauty, and holiness held within his single name, and its effect on our lives today.

The name of Jesus gives us access. The way to life is Jesus. Only Jesus. But for those in Christ, this doesn't equate to a small life. Instead, in Christ, life becomes larger, wider, more full of potential and blessing than any other way will ever allow us.

In the first half of this book we have been focusing on vision, on the wonders of living a wide-open, spacious life, and the sometimes difficult path that we must walk in order to get there.

But I think that far too often people mistakenly correlate the difficult path with being a restricting and constricting path—but the Bible doesn't say that! We read throughout the Old Testament that David's journey was at times intensely difficult, but in 2 Samuel 22:37, he says, "You enlarged my path under me; so my feet did not slip." The path may be difficult, and the gate may be narrow—but let me tell you, there is a whole lot of life to be accessed through that narrow gate! His name is JESUS. And as we step into grace and through the narrow gate, he leads us into a life of glorious potential.

The Way, the Truth, and the Narrow Gate

Why does this matter for us as we attempt to follow Christ and grow in our faith? Because there's one name that's foundational to our ability to live the big, abundant life God wants us to have: Jesus. We may not stop to think about the implications, the meaning, the power behind Jesus' name, but it's essential if we want to reach our divinely appointed destination. In fact, Jesus didn't leave us much choice. He said, "I am the way, the truth, and the life. No one comes to the Father except through Me" (John 14:6).

Notice Jesus didn't say that he's the tour director or the traffic cop for the way to know God. He said that he is the way. While I have no doubt that our path to knowing God is found only through Jesus, I also know that the message of the gospel is inclusive, not exclusive. Jesus invites everyone—men and women, Jew and Gentile, rich and poor, young and old, everyone—to accept the gift of grace by confessing that one and only name. While Jesus declares that he is the only way (exclusive), he opens his way up to all who call upon his name (inclusive). He's as inclusive as he is exclusive—it's the subversive nature of the gospel, the upside-down way of the kingdom, and good news for everyone.

So in order to enjoy the spacious, wide-open life Jesus came to bring and that we can access and enjoy in him, we have to believe him when he also said, "Enter by the narrow gate; for wide is the gate and broad is the way that leads to destruction, and there are many who go in by it. Because narrow is the gate and difficult is the way which leads to life, and there are few who find it" (Matt. 7:13–14). As I shared in the Introduction, this verse inspired me to write this book and served as its structural scaffold. Jesus makes it clear here that it's not going to be easy or convenient or popular to follow him. But as we'll see, I fear that sometimes we make the gate tighter and more confining than he does.

I'm getting ahead of myself, though. The key to unlocking the narrow gate is Jesus. There's no other name. Let's consider what makes his name unique and why it alone is more powerful than any other.

What's in a Name?

"Houston?"

"Present."

You know the drill. Countless times we have to give our name, acknowledge it, or answer to it. Depending on the difficulty others have with it, we may be used to spelling it for takeout orders and doctor's appointments. We may feel quite proud of our name and the family heritage it represents, or we may have changed our name from the one we were born with for a variety of reasons. We can't deny, though, that names carry great power by what we associate with them.

Most of us have a funny relationship with our names. We may not even think about them very often, but they usually serve as our point of reference for the people around us. We name people to distinguish them, to identify them, and perhaps to honor something larger (a family, a business, a heritage) of which they are part.

My name is Brian Charles Houston. I don't know exactly what my mum and dad were thinking when they chose the name "Brian." Charles was my maternal grandfather's name, and I never quite knew the weight of honor that carried until my eldest son had a boy and chose to name him Zion Alexander CHARLES Houston, after both of his granddads! Brian Charles Houston has served me well as far as names go. My identity is in my name, not spiritually speaking, but as I live out my life on earth as a man.

My credibility is in that name.

My reputation is in that name.

My authority is in that name.

To give someone else authority, my authority, I sign my name. Recognition is carried in my name. It does have some limitations, however. My name won't get me automatic access to Buckingham Palace or the White House.

But my name does get me in to certain places.

Recently my daughter and her little boy, Jack, my grandson, were flying out of Sydney on the same day that I was. Although we were going to entirely different destinations on different airlines, we had some time to spend together at the airport. At the time Jack was still nursing, so my daughter looked for a private spot, and so I suggested that she come with me to the airline's club lounge. Although they try to maintain a certain exclusivity, with my frequent travel schedule I sometimes feel as if the airport lounge is my second home, and I hoped they wouldn't mind if I brought along a guest who wasn't one of their passengers.

So we entered through sliding doors of frosted glass, past the doorman who always greets me with a smile, and immediately a familiar face looked up from behind the reception desk and smiled. Since honesty is always the best policy, I've found a direct approach is often the most effective. After the hostess and I exchanged pleasantries, I leaned in and said, "This is my daughter, Laura. She's actually not flying with me today—in fact, she's booked on a different airline's flight a little later. Do you think there's any chance she can join me in the lounge area?"

The lady looked at my daughter and little Jack and couldn't help but smile at the beautiful sight of a mother and child. "Well, Mr. Houston," she said apologetically, "we're really not permitted to do that...and I shouldn't even consider it, but for you, of course we can."

So my daughter was allowed to enter the exclusive lounge area and wait along with me in a quieter, more private setting. She couldn't do it on the power of her own name, but in this case my name got her in. In that instance, my name could get her places her own name could not. Of course, I know it won't be long until our roles are reversed, and I'll be telling everyone, "I'm Laura's dad. You know Laura, right? Well, I'm her dad."

But that day, her name and circumstance limited her ability to enter into this private lounge. She wouldn't have tried to gain entry on her own, because she knew the rules of membership.

However, since her dad was with her, I was able to gain entry for her.

Unfortunately, in life we often try to live according to the limitations of our name rather than understanding that the hope we have, the victory we have, the power we have, the promise we have, is in an entirely different name operating on a completely separate level. In other words, we often assume we can't do something because of our own limitations. We forget who made us and empowers us and can do anything.

You see, we can enter into the fullness of life, even though the gate is narrow, because we have the authority of the name of Jesus. There is not one thing in your life—no challenge, no problem, no heartache—over which you cannot speak the name of Jesus and see victory. Just as Laura gained access because she's my daughter, we belong to a family with much more clout, influence, and authority: the family of God.

The Unchangeable Name

Since we have started new churches around the world—in cities like London, Kiev, Dusseldorf, Paris, Cape Town, New York, and most recently in Los Angeles—we might be tempted to assume that the Hillsong name is drawing people. But this would be a huge mistake. The name Hillsong may initially attract people, but it will never save anybody!

Don't get me wrong; we're blessed to have a recognized name that God has graced, like Hillsong. It's our name and God has blessed us with this name. In fact, I know Hillsong is perhaps a bit of a weird name for a church. You might have guessed by now that it didn't emerge from the original Hebrew or Greek text, and you won't find Hillsong in the Bible. No, we pioneered our little church in an area of rolling hills in Sydney's Northwest called the "Hills District." It's about as simple as that.

When we began to produce our very first live worship albums I realized that people might not buy music titled "Hills Christian Life Centre Worship" (reflecting our original church name)—it just didn't roll off the tongue. So I got together with our team, and we sat and brainstormed what these projects could be called—and eventually everyone settled on "Hillsong." At the time, this brand encompassed our albums and our small annual music and creative conference—so each advertisement we put out would invite people along to these "Hillsong" events. But as both the worship and conference quickly gained traction, and more and more people came along, there seemed to be confusion about the name of the church. It wasn't uncommon to hear "Is this the Hills Christian Centre?" or "Hills Life Centre?" and "Is this those music people from the Hills?" Eventually people started saying things like "Are you going to that Hillsong Church?" until we got the hint and changed our name. And the rest—as they say—is history.

Hillsong is a name now recognizable not only in Australia but around the world! Little did we know that a small suburban church, locally nicknamed simply as "Hills," would spread so far beyond the district of its namesake.

Needless to say, we are proud to be part of this global church community, and we thank God that he's given us influence through the Hillsong name.

But the real influence, the real power source of every ministry ever attempted by Hillsong, has nothing to do with the name that is over the door of our church. The real influence and power source comes from the One who is our focus and Savior. Any impact we have comes from the Son of God, Jesus. He is who we worship, who we follow, who we look to guide us. His name is above every name and has power above every other name. It's never been about a church called Hillsong—it's always been about a Savior called JESUS!

The Oath

The Scripture says that in Bible times when someone made an oath, they found a name that had more authority, someone with more power, than themselves. If they made an oath in the name of this higher authority, then it was binding, and the higher authority then became responsible should the promise not be kept. So notice the unique promise God made to Abraham:

> For example, there was God's promise to Abraham. Since there was no one greater to swear by, God took an oath in his own name, saying: "I will certainly bless you, and I will multiply your descendants beyond number."
>
> Then Abraham waited patiently, and he received what God had promised.
>
> Now when people take an oath, they call on someone greater than themselves to hold them to it. And without any question that oath is binding. God also bound himself with an oath, so that those who received the promise could be perfectly sure that he would never change his mind. So God has given both his promise and his oath. These two things are unchangeable because it is impossible for God to lie. Therefore, we

who have fled to him for refuge can have great confidence as we hold to the hope that lies before us.

This hope is a strong and trustworthy anchor for our souls. It leads us through the curtain into God's inner sanctuary. (Hebrews 6:13–19 NLT)

Here we have an explanation that almost sounds like a legal document or something found in a courtroom. In a sense, that's exactly what it is, an understanding of the authority of God made manifest through his Son. God was speaking about blessing and fruitfulness, and to seal his promise he made an oath—which we often think of as swearing—on his own name. Because of our sinful nature, God knew there was a gap, a permanent separation, between his world and ours. So he sent Jesus to be the bridge for us to travel into God's kingdom.

And why did God make such an oath in his own name? Because there is no other name that is higher! There is no higher authority or greater name in the universe! In other words, his name gives us access into the things of God, access to the miraculous, into the supernatural. It takes us beyond the barricade and the limitation and into the presence of Almighty God.

The power of his name is continually echoed throughout Scripture. In Ephesians 1:21 we find his name "far above all principality and power and might and dominion, and every name that is named, not only in this age but also in that which is to come." And again in Philippians 2:9–11: "Therefore God also has highly exalted Him and given Him the name which is above every name, that at the name of Jesus every knee should bow, of those in heaven, and of those on earth, and of those under the earth, and that every tongue should confess that Jesus Christ is Lord, to the glory of God the Father."

The Bible also makes it clear that even demons have to recognize the power of the name of Jesus. His name causes all knees to bow and all tongues to confess the truth of who he is.

In the Jewish culture, the name Jesus literally means "Jehovah is salvation," which we often translate as "savior." The name came from God himself when he sent the angel to visit Mary with the amazing news that she would be the mother of God's Son. The angel told her, "Do not be afraid, Mary, for you have found favor with God. And behold, you will conceive in your womb and bring forth a Son, and shall call His name JESUS. He will be great, and will be called the Son of the Highest; and the Lord God will give Him the throne of His father David. And He will reign over the house of Jacob forever, and of His kingdom there will be no end" (Luke 1:30–33). So much meaning, power, history, and authority contained in that one name!

My name has limitations and so does yours. If we only live according to our own authority and influence, then we're always going to run up against our limitations.

That's why the only hope we have comes from the name of Jesus. His name is the narrow gate, and we have the right to live and operate under that great name above all names. This is the best news possible, especially regarding those problems for which we don't know the answers. We often face obstacles in life and feel squeezed off the faithful path of following Christ. We get so close to what the future holds, and yet we don't have any access to it. We can't find the trail that leads to this place God is calling us to reach, and we're not sure which next steps to take. That's where the power of Jesus' holy name becomes our key.

His name is strong, and yet tender. Fierce and yet gentle. It's trustworthy and sincere, powerful and merciful, and the declaration of its limitless ability could go on for eternity. The best news of all is that you and I have inherited it as joint heirs, brothers and sisters of Jesus. We have a legacy of power, purpose, and possibilities we've barely tapped into. The gate may be narrow, but Jesus always makes a way for those living under his oath of salvation, his promise—those traveling by his unchanging, unshakable name.

Do you want to know the way to get through the narrow gate? The name of Jesus—there is no other way, there is no other name!

CHAPTER TWELVE

Calling on the Name of Jesus

**Your Name is higher, Your Name is greater, all my
hope is in You,
Your Word unfailing, Your promise unshaken. All
my hope is in You.**

"Anchor," Hillsong Music, 2013

Jesus!"

Have you ever needed to cry out that name? Perhaps out of
either desperation or fear, you've been confronted with a situation
where you can think of no other name.

I have.

In the early days, our church was still meeting in a little school
hall in the northwest suburbs of Sydney—and my son, Ben, was
about two years old. After almost two years of growing consistently from week to week, we had packed that little school
hall where it all started for us, and we began to look for a new,
larger meeting space. It was a stretch, but we leased a brand-new
warehouse in the same area, which was becoming more and more
developed. The pastures and horse paddocks were being replaced
by businesses and warehouses like the one we rented.

I guess in those days occupational health and safety wasn't

monitored and regulated quite as closely as it is today, because our offices were located on a mezzanine floor upstairs above our meeting space, and while there was a railing around the stairwell, its posts were more decorative than substantial. There really wasn't much to keep someone from falling over or even sliding in between the rail posts.

So it was while I was sitting in my office one afternoon when I heard a sickening thud, one so hard it made the building momentarily tremble, from the stairs outside my door. Immediately, I thought, "Oh, please, Lord, I pray that wasn't Ben." As I said, Ben was probably between two and three at the time, and he would often visit the offices while Bobbie and I worked. Sure enough, when I ran out to the stairs, I saw Ben lying on the ground floor below, a cold concrete floor with no carpet or padding of any kind.

Galloping the stairs several at a time, I dashed to my son, my little boy, and realized he wasn't breathing. The sick feeling inside me collapsed in on itself, and I felt absolutely terrified. Each moment seemed frozen, as if I couldn't do anything for him fast enough. Ben's pale skin was growing even whiter, tinged with a bluish-purplish color. A small stream of blood trickled from the back of his tiny head, where I knew it had to be fractured.

Bobbie also had been at the church, and she came running when she heard the thud. We both felt so helpless and instantly responsible for not keeping a closer eye on him. We leaned over the still form of our son, whose skin glowed with an even stronger bluish tinge. Ben still wasn't breathing, and those few moments seemed like an eternity. I wasn't sure I should move him, but I also couldn't stand seeing him lying there on that cold concrete floor. So instinctively, I scooped him up in my arms and held him close to my chest as I screamed the only name I could utter, "JESUS!"

It was a prayer, a plea, and an urgent summons for help, the cry of a beggar pleading to keep the most precious gift he has—of a father who would take his son's place in an instant. Miraculously and immediately our little boy flickered his eyes and began to breathe again. I don't know whether it was the shock he got from such a loud scream, but I like to believe that it was truly the power that's in the only name I could call on in that instant.

It turned out that Ben did indeed cut his head and fracture his skull. In fact, he still has the scar to this day, next to a couple of other, newer scars from playing rugby and a few other extreme sports. But praise God there was no permanent damage done that day. I have no doubt that the only word I could utter, the name of Jesus Christ, saved him.

Beyond Silver and Gold

As any parent can tell you, sometimes the only thing you can do to help your child, whether they're young or fully grown, is to call on the name of Jesus. And you don't have to have children to call on the power of his beautiful name. You have only to believe, trust, and obey the loving voice of God as you travel through life's journey.

While we find numerous examples and demonstrations of the power of Jesus' name in the Bible, one of my favorite scenes occurs in Acts. In the third chapter we find a couple of Jesus' disciples on their way to the temple in Jerusalem to pray.

> Now Peter and John went up together to the temple
> at the hour of prayer, the ninth hour. And a certain
> man lame from his mother's womb was carried, whom

they laid daily at the gate of the temple which is called Beautiful, to ask alms from those who entered the temple; who, seeing Peter and John about to go into the temple, asked for alms.

And fixing his eyes on him, with John, Peter said, "Look at us."

So he gave them his attention, expecting to receive something from them.

Then Peter said, "Silver and gold I do not have, but what I do have I give you: In the name of Jesus Christ of Nazareth, rise up and walk."

And he took him by the right hand and lifted him up, and immediately his feet and ankle bones received strength. So he, leaping up, stood and walked and entered the temple with them—walking, leaping, and praising God. And all the people saw him walking and praising God. Then they knew that it was he who sat begging alms at the Beautiful Gate of the temple; and they were filled with wonder and amazement at what had happened to him. (Acts 3:1–10)

Among the many entrances to the temple, perhaps the most striking was this gate called the Beautiful Gate, or the Gate Beautiful. If you can imagine, it was seventy-five feet tall and made of bronze, with all kinds of ornate designs and elaborate scenes engraved into the thick metal. This gate was so heavy that it required twenty strong men just to open it. The first-century historian Josephus spoke about this gate and explained it was called Beautiful because it was beyond gold and silver in its dazzling, intricate splendor.

We're told this gate represented much more than just a beautiful entrance for a certain lame man, a beggar who, because he could not work, had been brought for forty years to sit beside the gate where many people passed and ask for money. For forty years, every day of his life, this crippled man was taken to the Beautiful Gate. He could sit there and beg next to it, but he wasn't allowed to enter into the temple courtyard like the many Jewish people who had a certain status. For all its magnificent beauty, this gate might as well have been a stone barricade or an iron curtain.

The lame beggar saw Peter and John about to enter the temple through the Beautiful Gate, and he called out to them for money, doing what he did there day in and day out. The two disciples noticed the man, asked for his complete attention, and then told him that they didn't have any money. "Silver and gold I do not have," Peter said. But then he gave the beggar something price-less, commanding him to rise and walk in the name of Jesus Christ of Nazareth.

Notice that Peter wasn't trying to live according to what he did not have. He knew that his own name, or John's, or anyone else's there in the city, did not have the authoritative ability to heal and to restore this man's lifelong ailment. But Peter knew what he did have: the power of Jesus' name. Too often we can get fixated on what we lack and forget what we actually do have. Through the name of Jesus, we have all we will ever need. Even though he had no money, Peter knew the precious worth of his Master's name. He knew the name of Jesus, like the Beautiful Gate of the temple, was beyond gold and silver.

Imagine being this lame man who'd been crippled for his entire life. He not only saw his feet straighten but he felt his ankles and legs strengthen. As Peter helped lift him up off the ground to stand on his own feet, the man discovered a state of physical health—pain-free legs—that he'd never known.

Suddenly he was testing his newfound strength and doing things he'd never done before—walking, skipping, and leaping. He could now go where he had never been able to go unassisted before that day. He had spent all that time, fourteen thousand days, being taken to the gate, and then for the first time he was able to go through the gate and finally enter the temple. With such healing power coursing through his body, this newly restored man had no choice but to praise God. Finally able to go through the Beautiful Gate, he could literally and figuratively enter into a deeper place of prayer, praise, and worship in the presence of God.

Peter told the man to get up and walk, and even went over to help lift the man to his feet. I love this detail, because it reminds us that Peter did what he could to assist this man in need, but Peter knew the real power for the man's healing could come only from Jesus. It's a lovely, concise picture of the role of the Church.

Our role is to lift people up, using our own strengths and abilities, so that the power of God through the name of Jesus Christ can heal them, restore them, and enable them to know God's love.

Many, many years ago as a young pastor, I realized that if my preaching and teaching was always aimed at building and lifting the lives of those I was speaking to—rather than being polarized around exhorting people to help me fulfill *my* vision and build *our* church—then Jesus would build *his* church. It has always been my goal to build not only people's spiritual lives but also their everyday lives—to preach to their Mondays, not just their Sundays. This includes lifting the lives of the broken and needy, reaching out to both the poor in spirit and the poor.

For years, our church has endeavored to see the need, both within our own walls and externally, in our local community and beyond. The need is great, but it has been the unhindered generosity of believers that has enabled the work of the kingdom and the name of Jesus to go forward into places we never could have envisioned or imagined.

Today, children in Mumbai are learning to read and write, are being fed and clothed and educated—and they are giving the next generation of their society hope for the future. Entire communities in Africa have been impacted through the generosity of the Church, and we've seen schools and houses, feeding programs and jobs, rise from the mud plains and poverty, bringing joy to families. Men and women have been saved, rescued, and prevented from entering the sex-trafficking industry as we've partnered with others to educate and prosecute people involved, and end this horrific crime against humanity.

The Church of Jesus Christ around the globe must be committed to seeing lives changed, families strengthened, cities transformed, and future generations positioned to make a difference. It is through this work that we have the opportunity to not only lift people's lives but to introduce them to the saving reality of Jesus Christ.

What we have to offer—the wonderful, beautiful name of Jesus—is far beyond and more precious than any silver or gold.

Name-Dropping

But the lame man's story of healing didn't end there, not by a long shot. Leaping and shouting with joy, this man went with Peter and John into the temple courtyard to a section known as Solomon's Porch (in Acts 3:10–11). When everyone marveled to see the lame beggar up and walking, Peter knew that he couldn't take credit for this miracle and wouldn't have dreamed of trying.

But giving credit to Jesus, who at this point had already been arrested, crucified, and resurrected, didn't go down so well with the Jewish religious leaders who wanted Christ killed in the first place. So it was no surprise that the guards known as the Sanhedrin, there at the temple gate, immediately arrested Peter and questioned him. They wanted to know what everyone there wanted to know: "How did you make this guy walk again? By what name? In whose power? In whose authority? What's really going on here?"

Peter made it undeniably clear that the only name capable of such a miracle is the name of Jesus. He said, "Let it be known to you and to all the people of Israel..." He proclaimed the power of the name of Jesus and wanted everyone there and then as well as here and now to recognize its limitless authority. As I indicated, Jesus was not a very popular person at that time, so his name was not one that Peter would try to name-drop to help get them out of this jam.

As a product of our human nature, we tend to love to name-drop—you know, mention the celebrities we've met, spotted at the airport, caught a glimpse of at our favorite restaurant, or sat next to at a charity dinner. Maybe in an effort to seem more glamorous and important or to pretend our lives are more exciting by association.

However, as Peter reveals, only the name of Jesus has the power to heal lives and to change hearts. Peter and John could not do it on their own any more than you or I could've healed that lame man. They knew what it meant, though, to pass through the narrow gate of a seemingly impossible situation. They knew what it meant to trust God for the impossible.

Through the name of Jesus, we have the same access to God's power that they had. Tragically, many times we live in the limitations of our name rather than in the freedom we have through the name above all names. We settle for less and assume we've reached our limits, that the best days of our lives are already behind us. And if we live only according to the name we're given or the name we choose for ourselves, then we face insurmountable limitations. Even if we're a famous celebrity, a notorious public figure, or royalty, we still have the limitations of our humanity.

Only one name elevates us beyond the limitations into which we're born. It's the name that can cause us to go where we've never gone; to do what we've never done or even imagined ourselves capable of doing. It's a name equally personal as it is powerful, as intimate as it is universal, both exclusive in being the only way to God and yet totally inclusive in its invitation to all people, both Jew and Gentile, male and female, slave and master.

The name of Jesus can unleash power in your life unlike anything you've ever experienced. It can open doors, close wounds, and reveal a path across the waters of a wind-tossed sea. His name allows us to burst beyond the limitations of our own names and our own abilities.

The hope we have in the name of Jesus is an anchor for our souls, a bridge both sure and steadfast uniting Heaven and earth. Our relationship with Jesus takes us straight out of this natural world and directly into the eternal realm of the presence of God. If we genuinely believe that his name is higher, that his word is greater, and that his power makes all things possible, then our anchor will keep us secure no matter how much the storms of life rage around us.

An Anchor for Our Souls

There is hope in the promise of the cross.
You gave everything to save the world You love.
And this hope is an anchor for my soul.
Our God will stand unshakable.

"Anchor," Hillsong Music, 2013

These lyrics were penned by two of our young songwriters here in Sydney, Ben Fielding and Dean Ussher. They began working on the song inspired by Hebrews 6:19, which says, "We have this hope as an anchor for the soul." Like many songwriters do, they walked away from the idea after getting stuck on lyrics and melodies and began working on other tunes.

Only a few weeks later, Dean and Rachel, now worship pastors at our Melbourne campus, tragically suffered a miscarriage, and this song became so much more personal. Both Ben and Dean knew that they had to finish what they started. Despite the circumstance, this Scripture had become a great reassurance in the midst of such loss and pain. Both songwriters committed to crafting the lyric around Hebrews 6. In God-orchestrated coincidence, I was scheduled to preach that week on the promise of God, his promise to Abraham and now to us.

Hebrews 6 treats our present hope and the unshakable nature of God's promise as inseparable. It speaks of two unshakable things: God's promise and his oath (his name). The hope that anchors the soul is the hope in the fact that God not only desires to fulfill his promise but is completely able to. He kept his word through the death and resurrection of Jesus. He has given us his name as a seal on his promise. His name is greater and higher than even the most overwhelming circumstance. When all is shaken, his word and the power of his name remains unshakable.

It is through the name of Jesus that you can find a new beginning and a new day, a new hope and a reassurance of a glorious future. God loves you and he is on your side. He sent his only Son to save you from your sins.

Yes, the gate is narrow but it is also beautiful. Through the power of Jesus' name, your foot is already in the door. Even when you fall and gasp for breath, one name holds the power of life. One name lifts you up again and again. One name is the anchor to our soul. One name holds the answers to sickness and death, holds the keys to blessing and future hope. Whatever your next step may be, whatever circumstances you might face, may the name you call upon be the One who will always answer: Jesus.

CHAPTER THIRTEEN

Discovering Narrow Is Never Tight

You hold the universe,
You hold everyone on earth.
"All I Need Is You," Hillsong Music, 2005

W̲hy would anyone want to see a movie about us?"

This was my response when some Hollywood producers approached Bobbie and me with a proposal for a Hillsong movie. We were in Los Angeles, where we had recently planted a new church, when we received a message through our media department back home in Sydney. Two gentlemen who were involved in the film industry had contacted our church and asked for a meeting with us. They were both well credentialed and well connected, and they offered to drive all the way from Hollywood to Orange County to meet with us. Bobbie and I were inquisitive, to say the least.

At lunch that day we were blessed to hear the most amazing story. I had met the first producer, Jon, briefly the year before, when he was visiting Australia promoting a Paramount Pictures movie. During his time down under, he visited Hillsong Conference and shared with us that day how deeply impacted he was by the people and the spirit of our church. He himself was a believer and had recently taken his fellow producer, Matt (our other lunch guest), to the Hillsong UNITED concert in the iconic Hollywood Bowl. That night may have been one of the only times that this esteemed venue had been filled with worship. He wasn't sure his friend would like the overtly Christian message but was eager to introduce him to music that meant a lot to him and to his faith.

So they went to the concert and found their seats way up toward the back of the eighteen-thousand-strong crowd. Only a couple of songs in, Jon turned to see, to his dismay, that Matt had disappeared. He assumed that his friend must not have cared for the dynamic music with the undeniable Christian message and had already left. "Oh, well," he thought, "I guess this wasn't his cup of tea—I hope he wasn't offended."

However, two hours later at the end of the concert, he looked up to see Matt running toward him. "Where have you been?" he asked. "I thought you left."

"No, I was down front!" Matt replied. "I can't explain it… there's just something so powerful about what happened tonight! I have never experienced anything like that."

As it turns out, like a high school kid, Matt had snuck his way down toward the front of the stage and stood captivated for nearly three hours of worship. As the producer of live stage productions such as *We Will Rock You*, he saw huge potential in the moment, and he began to tell us how he wanted other people to be able to experience what he had that night.

As we heard this story, Bobbie and I looked at each other and suppressed our smiles. They sure had our attention. Both men went on to describe their vision for a movie that would highlight some of the all-time favorite songs from our thirty-year journey, with behind-the-scenes insight into the songs, stories, and the songwriters, all through the lens of Hillsong UNITED. They clearly had put a great deal of thought into their pitch and seemed genuinely enthusiastic.

Bobbie and I shared their vision with the rest of our Hillsong team, and after some discussion, we began to move forward with the making of the movie *Hillsong: Let Hope Rise*. It was surreal to find ourselves in the offices of Hollywood distributors and financiers over the next few months, and interviewing potential movie directors—each of whom had built impressive résumés after directing some highly successful films. By God's grace, we saw all the pieces miraculously come together.

Sharing our journey from a school hall in the Sydney suburbs to a church graced with growing congregations in many of the world's great cities, the film gives viewers the opportunity to experience the impact of the praise and worship that God has birthed through Hillsong Church. We knew it would be hard work, particularly for the UNITED team and their families, not to mention the sometimes awkward situation of having cameras pointed at us constantly. Yet, when all was said and done, we could not pass on the opportunity to point others to the One we live for and long to glorify: Jesus.

Going to the Movies

Sometimes I have to shake my head in amazement at the days we are living in and the way the world has changed. To use a generalization, years ago many Christians spent their time and energy worrying about external practices and religious matters that really didn't have a lot to do with loving God and loving people! The judgmental attitudes of a small minority, who forced their perhaps well-meaning but ill-informed opinions on others, such as "no swimming on Sundays" or "rock-and-roll music is of the devil," ended up ostracizing and repelling many from ever entering a church building or calling upon Jesus' name. I grew up in an era when we were told by our church pastors, elders, and even parents that you shouldn't go to the movies in case "Jesus came again and you were in the movie theater." Apparently, Jesus didn't go to the movies! This example of small thinking does nothing for the gospel message, and even today we see these kinds of attitudes giving Christians a bad name.

If we live our lives in such a narrow way, believing what so much of the world continues to believe about Christianity—that it is meant to be kept small and quiet, represented by dilapidated buildings filled with narrow-minded, self-righteous finger pointers—then we will never find ourselves with all the opportunities that God can bring our way. Opportunities like a local church partnering with Hollywood in a culturally relevant way to spread the good news!

In the same way, films, multimedia, lights, and loud music aren't for everyone, and my firm belief is that relevance is not about the clothes you wear, the type of music you sing at your church, or the kind of car you drive. True relevance is measured by the distance between what you say and what you do. If your actions and lifestyle fail to line up with what you say, preach, and believe—then your message becomes irrelevant. I believe that if we live our lives in a wide-open way and remain relevant in terms of the definition above, we will see opportunities with spiritual eyes and attract the favor of God.

This means we cannot narrow our view of what serving Jesus looks like! What I've come to learn over many years is that the favor of God is sometimes unexplainable and outside of the box of the "safe" and "comfortable" Christianity some people seem to prefer. I don't for one minute believe that we need to conform to the world in order to make ourselves attractive to the unchurched; it is important to understand that the message (the gospel) is sacred, but I believe the methods have to change.

Open and Expansive

I have often said I'd rather be a musician than a music critic, a moviemaker than a movie critic, a chef than a food critic; and I'd rather be a church builder than a church critic. I would prefer to live my life as the kind of person who engages with the world of film and television, who spends money on the sound system so that Friday nights at youth group compete with any good party down the road, and who puts in the extra effort to graciously swing wide the doors of our church for activities during the week so that people who may never dream of coming to a Sunday service feel welcomed, loved, and cared for.

I love the way Paul spoke to the Corinthians about life with Jesus: "We didn't fence you in. The smallness you feel comes from within you. Your lives aren't small, but you're living them in a small way. I'm speaking as plainly as I can and with great affection. Open up your lives. Live openly and expansively!" (2 Cor. 6:11–13 MSG).

Open and expansive—or, in other terms, compassionate and embracing, gracious and all-encompassing. With social media so pervasive now, I continue to be amazed at the number of angry people who identify themselves as Christians but who have nothing positive, hopeful, affirming, gracious, or compassionate to say about anyone or anything. There are some particularly harsh and judgmental critics who seem determined to pick on people through Instagram, Twitter, Facebook, and comment forums, criticizing every form of faith and ready to publicly deride others with differing viewpoints.

My friend Phil Cooke calls people like this "armchair theologians"—those who hide behind their computer screens and look for "issues" to point out to fellow believers, all under the guise of biblical accountability. They see themselves as a kind of theological compass, ready to point out anything that seems amiss, off course, or simply not in line with their own understanding of the Bible. This isn't living openly and expansively at all, and more important, it bears no resemblance to the grace-filled way Jesus lived his life on earth. Ironically, Jesus saved his harshest words for the religious.

As a leader, I value the need for accountability and constructive feedback from colleagues and peers, from friends with relational and ministerial credibility who would take the time to reach out in care and correction. These conversations can make us better as leaders if we maintain a teachable spirit. It is probably wise to pay very little attention to the anonymous and mean-spirited attacks of those who may never have subjected themselves to accountability and correction. However, we must follow God's leading and not the whims of public opinion.

Whosoever Will

The truth is, this sour, narrow-minded, and mean form of Christianity from a small minority is nothing new. In fact, these are the kinds of people that the disciples encountered often on their travels—so critical of Jesus, looking for every opportunity to prove he wasn't God's Son. These are the same self-righteous religious leaders that Peter and John encountered after they healed the lame man begging next to the Beautiful Gate at the temple in Jerusalem. No sooner had they entered into the courtyard of Solomon's Porch, with the newly healed man jumping and leaping about, than others immediately began demanding to know how this was possible.

Being filled with the Holy Spirit, as well as being a passionate preacher-in-the-making, Peter knew he had everyone's full attention, and he took the opportunity to share the gospel:

> Men of Israel, why do you marvel at this? Or why look so intently at us, as though by our own power or godliness we had made this man walk? The God of Abraham, Isaac, and Jacob, the God of our fathers, glorified His Servant Jesus, whom you delivered up and denied in the presence of Pilate, when he was determined to let Him go. But you denied the Holy One and the Just, and asked for a murderer to be granted to you, and killed the Prince of life, whom God raised from the dead, of which we are witnesses. And His name, through faith in His name, has made this man strong, whom you see and know. Yes, the faith which comes through Him has given him this perfect soundness in the presence of you all. (Acts 3:12–16)

Once again, Peter makes it undeniably clear that it's not his power that has healed this lame man but the power of the name of Jesus. And to make sure that his audience got the message,

Peter explains the direct connection between "the God of Abraham, Isaac, and Jacob, the God of our fathers" and "His Servant Jesus." Everyone there in the temple would be there to worship and honor Jehovah, the Great "I Am" they had learned about as the one true God, the God of their people, the one who delivered the people of Israel from Egypt and led them to the Promised Land. But most of them had rejected Jesus as the Messiah, the long-promised Savior, and in part remained responsible for his arrest and death.

What I find so amazing here is the boldness Peter displays—he doesn't mince words! He basically acknowledges that the way to God is indeed through a narrow gate; after all, God is holy and perfect and people are sinful. But he tells them the same good news that we have to share with people around the world today: Jesus is the narrow gate and "whoever calls on the name of the Lord shall be saved" (Rom. 10:13).

"Whoever calls"—I love that phrase. Who am I to hinder the saving work of Christ by placing narrow restrictions on others?

For forty years the lame man had been taken *to* the temple gates, but for the first time ever he could enter *through* the temple gates—*go where he had never gone, and do what he'd never done*—walking, leaping, and praising God. This is exactly what life with Christ looks like—going where you've never gone and doing things that everyone said couldn't be done.

Going to the Church Graveyard

Only a few short years ago, I believe God spoke to me about the timing of planting our very first Hillsong Church in the United States. There has always been something about big cities with lots of people that has beckoned my attention. By God's grace, Hillsong Church is flourishing in all of the big, world-class cities where we are planted.

I knew, long before we ever began there, that New York would be one of those cities, and I've since learned that Carl Lentz and my son Joel (as twenty-one-year-olds in Bible college in Australia) had dreamed of one day starting a church together in NYC—a city that had previously been labeled a "graveyard" for churches. You see, despite the many great churches and pastors serving God already in this amazing "city that never sleeps"—where new nightclubs and restaurants are opening by the dozen—there are also many churches that are going "out of business." Many people warned us of this reality, and of the perils of planting in such an ungodly, transient, large city—and yet we knew that God had always opened doors for us if we were in tune with his Spirit, listening for his leading, and were in the right place, at the right time, with the right people.

Five years on, Hillsong New York City is thriving. We are consistently filling over seven services each weekend and seeing people line up around the block to hear the truth of the gospel. One of my favorite parts of Hillsong New York is seeing the diversity of the crowd each Sunday. From the faceless to the famous, the Word of God and passionate worship is touching people's lives in that city and changing them from the inside out. We are serving alongside other great churches and ministries in New York, and together we are seeing this concrete jungle and "church graveyard" come to life in the power of Jesus' name.

Paul told the Corinthians that "smallness" comes from within us, and not from God. The "smallness" we felt in such a big city could have hindered what God wanted to do if we had allowed it to navigate our thinking.

The truth is, the gateway to knowing God feels tight and constricting only when we try to do it on our own. When our human mind can't comprehend the miraculous work of Christ, then instead of allowing his grace and saving power to awe us, we criticize that which we don't know and shrink back from that which seems unknown. Rules, limits, regulations, and discipline become a burden only when we're forced to obey and understand in our own power, which we simply cannot do.

But through Jesus we have freedom and life, purpose and power, joy and peace. The narrow gate will never make you a smaller person—because you will never come second by putting God first.

When amazing things happen in our lives, some people may try to explain them away or find a "rational" reason. If they can't make sense of us because they have reduced the narrow gate to the size of a keyhole to match their own biases and limitations, then we must be gracious, loving, and respectful in response. We have to realize that in our everyday lives, through our churches, through the situations in which God places us, people will usually be confounded by a testimony that doesn't make sense to them. When we're part of something that's not the result of our own power, others can only scratch their heads.

And even when you're actively and accurately reflecting who Jesus is, even when you're revealing the wide-open, spacious life he brings as we pass through the narrow gate, some people will be drawn to God through you. They will realize something different about you, something that's not about who you are or what you're doing, but something supernatural, a glimpse of Christ. They are hungry to know God, so when we have the opportunity to heal, to preach, to teach in Jesus' name, we must not back down.

Others may try to silence you—either because they claim to know God but don't represent him truthfully, or because they don't know him and simply cannot understand the things of God. But because of the power we have through Jesus Christ, we will always be compelled to speak the truth of who he is and what he's done for us. Where God's Spirit opens doors, we must keep walking, knowing that the gate is narrow but not constricting. In other words, if someone approaches you one day about making your life into a movie that reflects what Christ has done—don't rule it out!

"So spacious is he, so roomy, that everything of God finds its proper place in him without crowding" (Col. 1:19 MSG).

CHAPTER FOURTEEN

A Holy Calling

**When You call I won't refuse, Each new day again
I'll choose
There is no one else for me, None but Jesus.**
"None But Jesus," Hillsong Music, 2006

In the early years of our ministry, when our children were young, Bobbie and I could hardly afford a vacation, let alone take time away from our small but growing congregation for one. Yet early on we learned the importance of time away with our children, and we began to make wonderful holiday memories even with our limited resources. I remember many summer days taking my boys out deep into the ocean waves and encouraging them to climb onto my back and hold on for dear life as we bodysurfed together to the shore. For a few days, the stress and pressure of being young pastors in a new country and planting a new church seemed to melt away in the heat of the sun.

On my worst days, I've thought how nice it would be to draw back, maybe get a job with no pressure. I've even watched somebody mowing a field on a tractor, with that beautiful aroma of freshly cut grass that accompanies spring, and I thought, "Imagine a job like that! When your biggest stress is whether or not you have enough gas to finish." Those thoughts never lasted long, though, because I had an overwhelming sense that I was to live called, not just saved.

God's Word says, "He has saved us and called us to a holy life—not because of anything we have done but because of his own purpose and grace. This grace was given us in Christ Jesus before the beginning of time" (2 Tim. 1:9 NIV). Are you content to live saved? Or is your commitment to live called? I believe "calling" takes away the option of simply "settling down."

There was an old pastor who pioneered a church in Sydney in the early 1920s or '30s, and he continued to minister, preaching and pastoring, well into his eighties. As the story goes, he had just finished preaching one Sunday morning, and the congregation closed the service with the hymn "Within the Veil I Now Would Come." And that was just what he did! The old preacher passed from this earth to Heaven right there in the same church he pioneered! Could there be any better way to go?

I admire his determination to his calling to share the gospel, and while I don't want to be doing all I do today in my eighties, I do pray that as long as I have breath I will live with a sense of calling and purpose. I want to find joy and passion in mentoring others, and setting up generations to build upon the foundations we (and those who have gone before us) labored to build.

Isn't this how you want to live your life? Filled with passion and excitement, with the confident knowledge that you're making a difference in the lives of others, contributing your efforts to God's kingdom for his eternal purposes? It's rarely easy, but I have always found it satisfying when I'm following the example set by Jesus, led by God's Spirit, fulfilling the purpose for which he made me. As we've discovered, this process is an ever-unfolding adventure, filled with unexpected challenges and miraculous surprises, both the trials and joys drawing us deeper in love with Jesus.

The only time I haven't enjoyed this level of satisfaction is when I've been tempted to settle for less than God's best or lost my vision for the future.

Personal Vision

Proverbs 29:18 says, "Where there is no revelation, the people cast off restraint." Another version says, "Where there is no vision, the people perish" (KJV).

We should never underestimate the significance of what we think about ourselves, the calling and purpose we hold on to that drives our lives forward. What is it that gets you out of bed in the morning? What is your personal vision for your life? When we don't have confidence in God's plan and purpose for our lives—when we walk through life without vision—we are walking a dangerous line.

Paul led a destructive life before his encounter with Christ on the Damascus road, before he entered through the narrow gate. Although he stayed his edgy self after his conversion, Paul's lifestyle was realigned so he would become a builder of the Church rather than a destroyer of it. Everything that was in him beforehand was bent on destroying the Church, but in Christ he found out what it was he was called to do; in Christ he found a personal vision.

Perhaps, like Paul, you think you've gone too far down the wrong road, made too many bad decisions to ever live a life of wisdom and discretion. Maybe you feel as if you've completely lost your way and can't find the way out, or maybe you've just made a few poor choices along the difficult road. Don't despair! It's *never* too late to make changes and choose again God's path for your life. His way is Jesus (see John 14:6) and his Word is the light that shows you the direction to go (see Ps. 119:105). God's grace will relocate you onto the right path and establish your life on a foundation that will stand in a time of storms and teach you how to make wise decisions for a glorious future.

Life is full of choices, and the choices you make will determine the course your life takes. But God's way—the narrow gate—will always point you in the direction of his purpose and fulfillment.

Looking Up, Looking Ahead

Often our hardest decisions are the small ones, the incremental ones, the choices that seem harmless enough in the moment. The big temptations we often identify and resist, but the really big issues of life usually begin with small choices. No one wakes up one day and thinks, "Today I'll settle for less," or "Today I'll take a break from following God and just wait and see what happens." No, instead the enemy tends to chip away at us in small moments of weakness. A shortcut here, a compromise there, a quick detour now and then—this is why we must remain focused on the example Jesus set for us.

Even though he came to earth on a mission as the Son of God, Jesus faced the same temptations that we face, including the temptation to settle. Our enemy tempted Jesus with the same opportunities to settle for less than God's best that the devil tempts us with today. The scale is different, but the essence of the temptation is basically the same.

In Matthew 4, the devil challenges Jesus to question his very identity. Twice he says, "If you are the Son of God…" Can't you just hear the taunt there? "If you're really who you claim to be, then you should be able to turn stones to bread and jump off cliffs!" But Jesus knows how to wield the Sword of Truth, and he resists the devil's attempt to test him. He responds with just the right counterpoint from Scripture to reveal the devil's shortsighted, warped logic. "Away with you, Satan! For it is written, 'You shall worship the LORD your God, and Him only you shall serve'" (v. 10).

I believe the tempter often challenges us with the same strategy in mind. If he can get us to doubt who we are and what we're doing, if he can cloud our vision, then he can get us to settle for less than God's best. He will cause you to question your calling, your best endeavors, and lead you into feeling condemned—questioning your identity in Christ.

These kinds of traps attempt to undermine where God is leading us. If we begin doubting our directions, our route, or our destination, then we'll usually stop to try and sort things out. But once we stop, then it becomes easier and easier to just go the easy way, the path of least resistance. Why worry about accomplishing something that seems impossible when you can just take it easy?

Jesus resisted the devil's temptations by relying on the truth of God's Word—our greatest resource. Whenever we begin feeling as if we're not talented enough or smart enough, that we don't have enough resources or enough support, that we should lower our expectations, then we must return to what God's Word tells us. The Bible assures us that we can do all things through Christ, that we are more than conquerors. God tells us that he will supply all our needs according to his limitless resources. We have to remember what's true and not start second-guessing what God has called us to accomplish.

Sometimes I believe following Jesus through the narrow gate is like Peter walking on water. As long as he kept his eyes on his Master, he could take the next step. But as soon as he looked down and realized how impossible it was for him to be doing what he was doing, then sure enough, he sank like a rock. If we keep our eyes on Jesus, then the gate is more than wide enough for us to pass through. But if we focus on how small the opening looks, or on all the directions others around us may be taking, then we lose sight of the gate.

Eyes up, one foot in front of the other.

Invent and Invest

In order to resist the temptation to settle, let's lead our lives so the fruits of our labor live long after our physical bodies have perished. In order to build God's eternal kingdom and leave this kind of legacy, we have to remain pioneers fueled by grace, committed to explore the wild territory to which God calls us, whether that's the kindergarten classroom, the mission field in another country, or the boardroom at our workplace.

Every field has its pioneers who dedicate their lives and careers to innovation and experimentation. It might be in a laboratory or on a laptop, in outer space or an inner office. It's the commitment to be the best you can be at what you're called to do. It's identifying your passions and pursuing them with a lifelong curiosity. It's leading when it would be easier to follow someone else and following God when you want to go your own way.

Pioneers take risks and take the first steps toward a new discovery, often an unknown one. They invent what they need as they go along, using the resources God provides and not dwelling on what they don't have. They step into something new, and they believe that God will keep his promises and provide the resources to realize the possibilities for greatness in their lives. Innovating, not settling for less, means allowing God to expand your imagination, increase your wisdom, and multiply your resources so that your energies can be sustained and extended. Not for your own glory, but for God's. When you serve God by leading a big life, it not only blesses you but provides opportunities for others to be blessed as well.

The mission of God at its finest is when we are quenching the deep thirst and ongoing need within the human soul. We lead a big life not for our own fame and fulfillment but so that we can lead others home, home to the house of God, the Church, here on earth and home to the eternal home awaiting us in Heaven. As long as you follow God's calling on your life and remain true to the pioneering wonder of his Holy Spirit, your life will overflow with joy, meaning, and God's very best.

Calling over Comfort

I was never content to settle when it was clear that Hillsong was Australia's largest church, because my goal as a church leader was never to build a church of a certain size or to gain notoriety from the accolade. It was always simply to do what God was calling us to do. Maintaining this mentality has seen us reach more people in more countries than we could have ever dreamed. And I still feel as if God is stretching me, stretching us, daring us not to settle or get too comfortable.

Hillsong has been nicknamed "the church that never sleeps." In many ways, it's a true depiction of a house that is always open, always moving from one event, one service, one location, to the next. We are always looking for the next thing, the new thing that God wants to do. When we stop to celebrate, it is a temporary pause, because we are not content to rest on the triumphs of the past but are always looking to the future.

Sometimes this way of living can cause a bit of friction. The continuous growth we have experienced over the years has inevitably brought with it growing pains. I will never forget the first Friday night gathering in Paris—the city of lights, the city of love, where historic cathedrals are visited daily by tourists, but rarely by worshippers. It's unknown to me at what point in history it happened, but as a country, France drifted far from God—more than 40 percent of the population claim they have no spiritual belief at all. But it didn't deter us from what we felt God was calling us to do.

Paris was to be our first-ever attempt at a Hillsong Church in Western Europe (beyond London), and I really didn't know what to expect. For years, a small group of people from Hillsong London labored and prayed over pioneering a contemporary Christ-centered church in Paris. It was always our long-term goal and belief that Hillsong London would make an impact on greater Europe, and this was the seed that enabled our first-ever gathering. Many people who knew Paris better than I did told me it would be a revival if even a hundred people turned up in such a "godless" city.

On the evening of our first meeting, Gary Clarke, our London lead pastor, and I caught a cab to the venue that was less than a block from the Pompidou Centre and only a short distance from the Louvre and the river Seine. As we got one or two blocks from the square, a lineup of people appeared in the distance, standing in the cold and winding around the block. I turned to our host and asked what these people were lining up for. I was astonished to discover that they were trying to squeeze into the small theater we had rented. It was impossible to get everyone in, and to this day I don't know where all those people came from! Even a reporter and a cameraman from a major Australian newspaper were there to report Hillsong's expansion into Europe and record what was a historic night.

I left that evening with a new inspiration and insight into the spiritual climate and hunger for truth in Europe, the same hunger we have seen replicated from Barcelona to Amsterdam and Stockholm to Dusseldorf. Our continuous prayer is that we will see a spiritual revival ignite in Europe.

After that first night we had to get about the business of turning a crowd into a church, finding out who was there for the long haul. We had to find consistent, affordable, and suitable places to gather and build DNA and culture into the leadership team. Since that first night we have had to work hard to build a church filled consistently with faithful people; but today, in many of our Hillsong Church campuses, we are creating entire teams of volunteers who are adept at managing lines—accommodating people who sometimes will wait for hours outside until the next service.

To this day, lines have become a feature of so many of our congregations as buildings struggle to contain the growth. Whether outside the Dominion Theatre in London's West End, or outside the Hammerstein and the Manhattan Ballroom in midtown Manhattan, or even outside the Belasco Theater bringing new life to downtown Los Angeles. These are problems we never imagined we would have, and that those who have gone before us prayed for... good problems, growing pains. In many ways, these growing pains don't give us room to settle because they require miraculous answers and provision, day to day.

The stretch on new leaders, the urgency to create volunteer teams and disciple new Christians are the kind of struggles that can become overwhelming and, at times, uncomfortable. Yet when things get uncomfortable we can choose to focus on the end goal: salvation, discipleship, and God's glorious future.

I encourage you—no matter how difficult the path gets, how distant the vision, how uncomfortable the stretch—to choose calling over comfort.

Planted and Flourishing

Your calling and vocation are at risk of being swayed, uprooted, or led astray during these inevitably uncomfortable moments if you are not grounded in truth and watered by accountable relationship and encouraging teaching. If you want to cultivate the kind of big life modeled by Christ, if you want to flourish in your personal vision and calling, and enter into a glorious future, then it requires putting down deep roots. This is a biblical truth we find throughout Scripture.

In God's Word, we are frequently compared to trees in how we live our lives and respond to the gift of our Father's grace. "For he shall be like a tree planted by the waters, which spreads out its roots by the river" (Jer. 17:8). "The righteous shall flourish like the palm tree: he shall grow like a cedar in Lebanon. Those that be planted in the house of the LORD shall flourish in the courts of our God" (Ps. 92:12–13 KJV).

For me, when it comes to flourishing in your calling, church is a nonnegotiable. I recognize that church looks different for everyone, but planting yourself in a community of believers who can build up, challenge, and encourage you in your calling is imperative. And I'm not talking about just being a "show-up-on-Sunday Christian." Just like the tree, if we are to flourish and produce fruit, we have to have our roots down deep in order to receive regular nourishment. Being present and building meaningful relationships with other believers has a significant impact on both our relationship with God and our future.

For many people, finding their place in the family of God is where they will also discover their calling, or gain a sense of purpose in their vocation. But don't be discouraged if this takes time, or you are not yet feeling planted or fruitful. It's hard to stand in front of any tree and actually see it growing before our eyes. Life, faith, and serving Jesus is like that; we can't always see what God is doing in the present moment, but we have to trust that if we are being faithful to steward our calling, he is providing all we need to continue growing.

Just like a tree, a flourishing life is a fruitful life; it will show signs of growth and health: foliage, fruit, flowers, and seeds in abundance. The tree itself will become strong and resilient, rising above the storms of life to also provide shelter for others.

When we live according to the purposes of God, when we don't simply live saved, when we plant ourselves in the good "soil and water" of godly relationships, sound teaching, and the truth of God's Word, we will see the fruit of our lives produce more than we could ever imagine. When our vision is clear and we don't settle for less than God's best; when we refuse to listen to the lies of the enemy and walk through the narrow gate, confident in our calling, we will find life in abundance—a glorious future. Paul really sums it all up in Ephesians 1:11: "It's in Christ that we find out who we are and what we are living for" (MSG).

A holy calling.

A glorious future.

CHAPTER FIFTEEN

A Jesus Generation

**I see a generation rising up to take their place,
with selfless faith.**

"Hosanna," Hillsong Music, 2007

I grew up with pastors for parents, and our home was so often filled with guest evangelists and preachers who were ministering in New Zealand and required hosting. On one particular occasion, a friend of my mum and dad, an evangelist from Fiji, was staying at our home and decided to do an impromptu Bible study with my little sister and me. I remember he opened the Bible to Matthew 1 and began reading out loud forty-two generations of family names, from Abraham to Jesus.

As a child, I could barely understand the lesson and study he gave that day, but I have never forgotten his enthusiasm. It was so obvious to me that he could see and understand something that I could not. Years on, I can understand the significance of what those names represented: a promise fulfilled.

When Abram was ninety-nine years old, the LORD appeared to Abram and said to him, "I am Almighty God; walk before Me and be blameless. And I will make My covenant between Me and you, and will multiply you exceedingly." Then Abram fell on his face, and God talked with him, saying: "As for Me, behold, My covenant is with you, and you shall be a father of many nations. No longer shall your name be called Abram, but your name shall be Abraham; for I have made you a father of many nations. I will make you exceedingly fruitful; and I will make nations of you, and kings shall come from you. And I will establish My covenant between Me and you and your descendants after you in their generations, for an everlasting covenant, to be God to you and your descendants after you. Also I give to you and your descendants after you the land in which you are a stranger, all the land of Canaan, as an everlasting possession; and I will be their God." (Genesis 17:1–8)

We don't have to wait long when reading through the Bible to find God's generational promise to his people, his generational promise to *you*. God uses generations, works through generations, and is undeniably committed to the generations. The faithfulness of our God is not confined to a generation, but it passes from one to the next. The very purpose of God choosing Abraham and his descendants was so that God might be made known, evidenced through their lives and witness. God has proven himself since his first promise to Abraham, and we have seen it outworked in the generations that followed.

Centuries later, the death of Jesus Christ on the cross and his resurrection delivered us this message of generations. As believers, when we choose to walk through the narrow gate, we stand as heirs to this very same promise made to Abraham. God promised

Abraham that his goodness and blessing would be recognizable, and that same promise extends to our generation and the generations to follow. God still chooses to build into generations—and I believe it is through the power of community, the intimacy of relationship, and the vehicle of the Church that he is continuing to reveal who he is to the world.

His continued promises are both personal and universal, directed to individual lives forming his Church, the Body of Christ. God's promises extend beyond the personal ones we have in our hearts and unite us all in the hope we have in Jesus.

In the Body of Christ, we are all connected in a great network of spiritual relationships, and God uses us—one generation after the next—to help each other along the path of faith and through the narrow gate.

Power of Partnership

Individual success is an illusion; anyone who claims sole credit for the successes of life allows pride to deceive them. Behind even the most seemingly individual triumphs there are coaches, teachers, lecturers, family, friends, mentors, an opportunity created by another. Dependability leads us into community and not away from it. It is in community (relationship and partnership) that we discover the needs of others, and we respond by being dependable and trustworthy stewards of what we have been given, good stewards of our holy calling; the result is then thanksgiving and community with God. When we are in relationship with our Heavenly Father, God gives us his Spirit to empower and equip us to do what he would do.

The fact is, our God is all-sovereign, all-powerful, and able to do absolutely anything, and yet he chooses to use us, to lean on us. And I believe that when we lean on and in to others, open our hands and open our lives, God smiles. Because he sees that we have learned something of who he is and what he intended.

I am a great believer in the power of partnership. At Hillsong Church there is an incredible emphasis on being a people known for turning generously toward need and never away from it, for choosing each other over individuality. Years ago, an amazing family came into our church. Barry and Lynn Denton had four boys, and they began attending Hillsong out of a desire to surround their children with a strong peer group and an active youth ministry.

Many years on, when these boys had become young men and begun businesses of their own, two of the brothers made a decision to stretch themselves and begin a development company; their professional skills complemented each other, and their vision for the future was cohesive.

At this time our church had been growing rapidly, and it was proving impossible to find anywhere consistent to gather. We were a young congregation, financially stretched, and I needed a God-idea, to hear from the Holy Spirit about how to move forward. I knew it was unlikely that anybody in our congregation could give that amount of money themselves, but one hundred of us together could take part in a million-dollar miracle. One evening at our first-ever men's retreat, one hundred men gathered around me to pray for this provision and commit what seemed like a distant miracle to Jehovah Jireh—the Lord, Our Provider. Two of those men were the Denton brothers. Their love for God and commitment to build his House led them to align their calling to a greater cause—and they attached their vision to ours.

In fact, the Hillsong Church vision statement begins with the words "*To reach and influence the world* by building a large, Christ-centered, Bible-based church..." And the vision for the Denton Brothers' company is, "*To reach and influence the world* by creating wealth through Kingdom principles for Kingdom purpose." And that is exactly what they are doing—living out the principles that they have learned in church.

Today, their successful business buys large parcels of land in Queensland, a beautiful, subtropic part of Australia that boasts the Great Barrier Reef as one of its many jewels. A few years on from that original prayer, the two brothers' skills and hard work, accompanied with their determination and faith, resulted in their business partnership giving one million dollars to the work of the church in a single year. This is the power of partnering with generosity in mind. To this day, those men are not only an integral part of our church leadership team, but their spouses, children, nieces, and nephews serve across the breadth of the Hillsong family—living and leading a life of example. Their choice to partner with our church and, ultimately, the will of God for their lives, along with their generosity on a practical level, has undoubtedly left a mark on the future generations who will walk through our doors.

I believe your success and effectiveness in life, love, and leadership hinges on your ability to partner with the strategically placed people alongside you for the adventure—people who are willing and able to carry the vision, run the race, and serve Jesus together. A generation of relationships and partnerships marked by God for future calling and undeniable purpose—a Jesus generation.

Honor the Past, Build for the Future

Our ability to blaze a trail for others relies on those who have gone before us. Ultimately, we can trace it back to those first followers of Jesus in the early church. They had no idea they were launching a movement that would change the course of history for centuries to come; they were simply being obedient and following as God's Spirit directed them.

A number of years ago, just a few short months apart, I visited the former churches of two very prominent world-renowned pastors who had graduated to Heaven. Both of these churches now had their sons at the helm, entrusted with the leadership and momentum of their flourishing ministries. One of the sons I had the opportunity to visit with (and subsequently form a relationship with) has honored his father every step of the way, while quietly getting about being true to himself and changing so much of what his father had established. The result has been staggering growth and influence for their ministry. The other, however, tried desperately to keep his father's name and ministry alive and tried to prop up the past, rather than build for the future. As I spent time there, it was startling to see everywhere the sad reminders of past days of blessing—and to look around and realize that present momentum had come to a grinding halt and things were clearly lacking life and forward motion.

The difference? One honored the past but built for the future. The other lacked vision for the future and tried to rekindle the past.

The truth is that the message of Jesus Christ is timeless, and it is as relevant today as it was some two thousand years ago. However, the challenge for all of us is this: How do we ensure that this generation hears the message in a relevant way—in the midst of the thousands of other voices vying for their attention?

In 1 Chronicles 12 we read about the armies of David preparing for battle. God had revealed that the time was right for David to overtake Saul, and in this particular account, the writer traces through the genealogy of David's army and the tribes that served him. I love the way he describes the sons of Issachar in verse 32: "the sons of Issachar who had understanding of the times."

Just like the sons of Issachar, we need to understand our times and know what we ought to do if we are going to effectively reach this and future generations. In other words, we need to stay relevant and in touch with a dramatically changing world without compromising the integrity and power of the message of Christ.

I remember talking to my daughter, Laura, a number of years ago, about Hillsong UNITED. They were once a youth band, but their lives have since grown; now many of them have children of their own, yet they're still fulfilling their dreams, breaking records, and innovating new sounds and lyrics for worshippers throughout all the continents in the world. Deep in my spirit, despite the continued success of Hillsong UNITED, I felt that it was time to pioneer again with a fresh Jesus generation—something that would connect with the hearts of young people still of school age.

It started late one evening in the summer, after an appointment at our City Campus on a Friday night, when I walked into rehearsals for Wildlife—our youth group for high schoolers. I was amazed by the young seventeen-year-old standing on the stage leading worship as though there were thousands in the room, though in reality the auditorium was absolutely empty. I went home inspired to tell Laura who, along with her husband, Peter, are our youth pastors. As I described my experience, she told me that Aodhan, the young man I had seen, was not only a worship leader but also a songwriter. That night I had seen him rehearsing one of his own songs. In a sense, it was at that moment, and in that conversation with Laura, that Young and Free was born.

Young and Free is a vibrant band, once again built from the talent within our own youth. It has fresh sounds and willing and wide-eyed Jesus-loving young people, who are sparking a whole new movement among teenagers and young adults. Their worship has brought fresh life into our own church and an incredible sense of excitement as people watch the generations grow stronger.

I have always said that I want our church to be the kind of church that is committed to empowering the generations and releasing them to do even greater things than my generation, or those that have gone before. Psalm 45:16 says, "Instead of Your fathers shall be Your sons, Whom You shall make princes in all the earth."

Instead of your fathers shall be your sons. I believe as a church we are called to be making princes in all the earth—kingmakers. We are to be bringing people, both men and women, young and old, inside the body of Christ into their God-given destiny; helping them to live a wide-open, spacious life and build toward a glorious future. We are to take the message of Jesus and see his kingdom move forward, stronger, into each generation.

If you think about fathers in terms of what is known, expected, proven, and established then you can think of sons as the opposite. Sons are unproven, untried, unknown, uninitiated, unpredictable. Our human nature tells us to stick with that which is established and proven. Yet I believe God wants us to keep pushing toward what is unknown and uninitiated, to look forward with a spirit of unpredictability and a spirit of adventure.

Don't get me wrong—we have a responsibility to honor our fathers, care for our fathers, love our fathers...but we have an obligation to the sons. I have a deep sense of gratitude for those who have partnered with Bobbie and me through all the seasons of church life. Through the highs and the lows, the joys and the sorrows, the seasons of momentum and utter frustration. But I have also seen way too many ministries age, blissfully unaware of their shrinking impact, influence, and relevance as their environment ages along with them. I'm determined not to allow that to happen. We need to honor the past, but also build for the future. Connected to the world we live in, but positioned in a way that brings hope, love, and answers to people of all walks of life and experiences.

People are not looking for stale religion; they want to know that God can make a difference in their lives, their families, their relationships, and their workplace today—and he can! If we have a generational focus in all that we do, our faith will continue to surge forward, and countless lives will continue to be indelibly changed.

I was recently thinking about this in relation to Psalm 44. Here the sons of Korah reflect on the good old days, the days when God was with their forefathers, in contrast to the days they were living in now, when they felt God had forsaken them.

In this Psalm they exclaim: "We have heard with our ears, O God; our ancestors have told us what you did in their days, in days long ago. With your hand you drove out the nations and planted our ancestors; you crushed the peoples and made our ancestors flourish" (Ps. 44:1–2 NIV).

What will the coming generations say when they look back in history to the twenty-first century? Will they, like the sons of Korah, marvel at the move of God, the progress of the Church, and the advancement of the kingdom? I certainly hope so. I believe we have a responsibility to the legend and legacy we will leave the coming generations. We have no control over how the future generations will steward what is given to them, but we can set them up to win by teaching them how to "Love God, Love People, and Love Life."

If our earnest commitment as individual believers and leaders is fulfilling this and teaching others to do likewise, I believe the Church will never fade into insignificance.

The Future Awaits...

As we all play a part, the Church will continue to grow stronger. Its foundation is Jesus, its hands and feet are you and me, and its future is those who are yet to come. Think about it: When we share the gospel with our neighbor or the lady at the supermarket checkout, we are not only sharing with that one person but with their family—and quite possibly their families' families. When we give generously, we do what Jesus said he was doing—building his Church. We build his Church so that those who are not yet living the wide-open, spacious life, who have not yet passed through the narrow gate, might come to know the God of all the ages.

I love watching God pick people up out of a life of sin and despair, and not only turn their lives around, but turn others around through them. Brenden is one of those.

Brenden grew up as an altar boy in the Catholic Church, yet at the age of fourteen, a seventeen-year-old friend offered him drugs and alcohol at a party. And that was where it all began... weekend after weekend, party after party, and substance after substance, his life spun out of control. By his early twenties Brenden was living recklessly, and his life was filled with uncertainty and emptiness. Lacking purpose, he delved deeper into the world of partying and became the manager of a nightclub where his destructive habits were not only fed but encouraged.

One night, at the young age of twenty-three, Brenden stumbled out of a nightclub after taking a lethal mixture of substances. He recalls how everything was spinning; he couldn't breathe and felt enveloped by the fear in his heart as he realized that he might have gone too far. Brenden describes sitting down in a dirty gutter, empty bottles and garbage at his feet, struggling to maintain control as his body manifested the destruction of his overdose. His body trembled and his heart pounded as he looked past the city lights into the night sky and cried out, "God, if you're real, I'm scared. Please help me get out of this place—I'm too young to die!"

God not only answered his prayer, but over the next six months he brought people into Brenden's life who shared with him the story of God's love, hope, and redemption. People who loved him and told him that God also loved him, just the way he was. In March 2001, two of Brenden's friends invited him to attend church—our church.

Brenden recalls the lines outside of our hub auditorium and remembers thinking, "What kind of place is this? I've seen lines for nightclubs, but never a church!" That night he encountered God and responded to the salvation altar call, opening his life to the saving work of Jesus Christ. Over the next number of years, I had the privilege to watch Brenden not only change his lifestyle but also attend Hillsong Bible College and contribute so much to the life of our church. Brenden's passion to see other people's lives changed has led him to share his story and the gospel with countless others—including his own parents, his only brother, and ultimately the beautiful woman who became his wife.

I watch with great joy now as Brenden and Jacqui pastor our Burwood campus in western Sydney and continually bring new people to church; their two young sons worship with outstretched arms in our kids' programs, and their own families have not only found Jesus but also serve in the House of God. An entire family legacy changed by the powerful story of one encounter, one invitation, one decision.

You see, we must not simply build only for what we immediately see, but for the potential in generations unborn, those who have not yet met Jesus, who will one day sit in our seats, stand on our shoulders, and do greater things than we have ever done.

Today, keep the future in your sights. Make the decision right now to choose the pathway of blessing that God has laid out for you in the Bible, the Holy Calling, and the narrow gate, so that long after you have gone, your legacy of blessing will live on in the generations to come. Honor the past, live for today, and build toward a glorious future!

> One *generation* shall praise Your works to another, and shall declare Your mighty acts. (Psalm 145:4; emphasis added)

PART 4

A Glorious Future

CHAPTER SIXTEEN

A Robust Kind of Faith

My faith is in things unseen
Bringing life where it has not been
Speaking things that were not, as if they were
I am alive in You.

"All Things New," Hillsong Music, 2014

Granny Diamond was old. Very old.

Part of the greatest generation, she came of age during the Great Depression, a reality that shaped this tough little lady into the woman that she was. When I first met Granny Diamond, she was elderly and tiny in stature—I think I outgrew her when I was about ten years old. She was frail and bent over, but boy did she have a good set of lungs! The church where I grew up in Lower Hutt, New Zealand, was a vibrant church with several hundred worshippers every Sunday morning—still, there was always one voice you could hear above every other: Granny Diamond. She was always a bar or two ahead of everyone else, and by the pitch and pace of her melodic hymns, you could always tell that Granny Diamond was in church, even though she was far too short to actually be seen!

I remember hearing a story about Granny Diamond that

perfectly describes her posture of faith. Apparently, she collapsed on the railway station platform one day many years ago as she awaited her train home. Bystanders were quick to call the ambulance, and within minutes the medics were on the scene, kneeling over this tiny and seemingly fragile woman. But Granny Diamond didn't want a bar of it. Though she lay on the train platform gasping for breath, she began to sing and worship at the top of her lungs. Fighting off the bemused paramedics, she got to her feet and finally walked all the way home, still singing and praising her God.

Granny Diamond's faith was muscular, gutsy, and robust—the kind of faith that left an impression on a young boy. She finally died just short of turning a hundred years old, and I imagine all of Heaven can hear her praising, slightly out of time and a little out of tune, but louder than all the Heavenly host.

Robust faith has very little to do with physical stature or strength but everything to do with spiritual muscle. I'd imagine that Granny Diamond is among the character of the kind of people we find listed in Hebrews 11, often called the "Faith Hall of Fame." These people displayed the type of faith you need to enjoy all that awaits you in your God-given purpose, the type of faith needed to live saved, called, and fulfilling the glorious future for which you are graced.

Hall of Faith

Cataloging almost every incredible person and his or her story from the Old Testament, Hebrews 11 begins by simply defining its focus: "Now faith is the substance of things hoped for, the evidence of things not seen. For by it the elders obtained a good testimony" (v. 1–2). These elders of the faith included Noah, Abraham and Sarah, Jacob, Joseph, Moses, Rahab, Samuel, and David, among many others. Their "good testimony" is the legacy of faith they left, the story of how they trusted God in the midst of overwhelming ordeals and obstacles.

Clearly, it wasn't their own power that fueled these individuals' victories. But it was actually out of their weaknesses that God enabled them to do amazing feats: conquer kingdoms, overcome lions, quench fires, dodge swords, and win battles when overwhelmingly outnumbered (Heb. 11:33–34). Sounds to me like pretty gutsy faith! I don't know about you, but I could often use courageous faith like that. Guts to share my faith, guts to do the right thing, guts to live well, lead well, and love well. Guts to stand up in the face of challenges and hold firm to God's promises.

The Bible frequently talks about this fight of faith. It's when you have no resources or opportunities, no solutions of your own, nowhere else to turn when you're in a battle, that you're forced to trust in God's ability to provide and meet you in your need. If nothing ever went wrong in life, then we wouldn't need to rely on faith or trust in God. We might as well be living in the Garden of Eden again. But that's not where we are—we live in a world contaminated by human sin, a world of temptation and disappointment, a world that God saved through the gift of his Son's sacrifice on the cross. Therefore, we're called more than conquerors (Rom. 8:37), reflecting the truth that we are called to fight a battle of faith throughout our lives. Are you capable of that kind of faith? Are you ready and armed for the fight?

Sometimes it's easy to have faith when everything is going great, but courageous faith—robust faith—is forged only when it's tested.

Subdued Kingdoms

Joshua's faith was tested. In fact, Joshua 1 starts with an announcement from God:

> Moses My servant is dead. Now therefore, arise, go
> over this Jordan, you and all this people, to the land
> which I am giving to them—the children of Israel.
> Every place that the sole of your foot will tread upon I
> have given you, as I said to Moses. From the wilderness
> and this Lebanon as far as the great river, the River
> Euphrates, all the land of the Hittites, and to the Great
> Sea toward the going down of the sun, shall be your
> territory. No man shall be able to stand before you all
> the days of your life; as I was with Moses, so I will be
> with you. I will not leave you nor forsake you. Be strong
> and of good courage, for to this people you shall divide
> as an inheritance the land which I swore to their fathers
> to give them. Only be strong and very courageous, that
> you may observe to do according to all the law which
> Moses My servant commanded you; do not turn from
> it to the right hand or to the left, that you may prosper
> wherever you go. This Book of the Law shall not depart
> from your mouth, but you shall meditate in it day and
> night, that you may observe to do according to all that
> is written in it. For then you will make your way pros-
> perous, and then you will have good success. Have I not
> commanded you? Be strong and of good courage; do
> not be afraid, nor be dismayed, for the LORD your God
> is with you wherever you go. (Joshua 1:2–11)

Joshua must have been waiting for this call-up for some time. In this passage, the Lord was saying to Joshua, "Moses is dead, and it's your time! All of this land will be yours."

You see, Joshua led Israel in the conquest of the Promised Land. He was a military commander and a national leader. As an aide to Moses, he was being prepared for this moment long before it ever happened. I think God does that. He was teaching Joshua what he needed to know to become a godly leader— knowing full well what was in his future. Joshua's earlier training demonstrates to us how God can use your life experiences to equip and prepare you before calling you to do even greater things. Preparation for a glorious future.

So when Joshua received his call, it should have been so exciting, so accessible—except why did God need to keep telling him to be strong and courageous? Was he missing something? In fact, he was missing thirty-one somethings!

You see, Joshua had thirty-one kings in his future—thirty-one kings he needed to defeat in order to enter into the Promised Land. Each and every one of these kings were the unmentioned barriers or, more accurate, *mountains* that Joshua would need to move in order to possess the glorious future promised to his people.

Mountain-Moving Faith

The Bible talks about faith that is strong enough to move mountains. Now that would take some strength! Jesus says in Matthew 21:21–22, "Assuredly, I say to you, if you have faith and do not doubt, you will not only do what was done to the fig tree [he had just cursed and withered a fig tree], but also if you say to this mountain, 'Be removed and be cast into the sea,' it will be done. And whatever things you ask in prayer, believing, you will receive."

It's a pretty crazy thought. I don't know about you, but I would love to move a few mountains around. I used to love going snowboarding. I think one of the first things I would do with this kind of faith is move the biggest mountain in Australia (7,310 feet) to France, and I'd move the French Alps down here to Australia. But I'm sure that's not what Jesus meant.

What he meant is that we will all encounter problems that become like mountains in our lifetime. Perhaps you can think of the mountains that are currently right in front of you. Maybe your mountains or your thirty-one kings have names like "debt," "marriage breakdown," "depression," or "cancer."

Sometimes our problems feel like a mountain filling the entire windshield of our car, obstructing the view and blocking our vision of the path ahead. The only remedy, the road map to traversing the rocky pass, coming around the last bend and seeing that mountain recede into the distance in your rearview mirror, is through holding on to God's Word and standing strong in your faith. These "mountain treks" are what testimonies are made of. What was once ahead of you, a seemingly impossibly large, rocky, slippery, and threatening mountain, has moved and is now behind you through the power that's in Jesus' name.

In more than thirty years of ministry, I've faced some serious mountains, many of them mentioned earlier in this book. I've come under fire from the press, faced disappointments with people, had a crisis of confidence, family challenges, and financial hurdles. Just like Joshua, I believe it is when there is land or territory at stake that faith comes with a fight. If you are facing a mountain, be encouraged—if you are gaining land, the devil is losing it, and the forces of darkness that are arraigned against God's promises hate losing territory. Faith is the answer, and robust and ready faith is the key. Because the only way to defeat thirty-one kings is one at a time.

Robust and Ready

In order for our faith to endure over the long haul and in the midst of setbacks and challenges, we must exercise and strengthen it. The kind of faith required to survive life's harshest blows must be strong, muscular, robust, and resilient. The word *robust* means "strong and healthy; hardy and vigorous." Once we have made the commitment to follow Jesus and live the Christian life, we sometimes overlook our ongoing need to exercise and practice what we believe. But our spiritual muscles are very much like the ones in our bodies that need development on a regular basis in order to grow and remain strong and healthy.

Without regular physical exercise, our muscles atrophy—they shrink and weaken to the point that they no longer function properly. If we don't exercise our faith on a daily basis, then it becomes weak and limp, unable to stand up to the trials and temptations we inevitably face. People who strengthen their faith and grow in their love and trust of God know that it requires the right focus. They know we have to keep our faith in Jesus, not in other people or in material possessions or even in the Church.

Grounded in your relationship with Christ, your faith grows over time with every new challenge, battle, or obstacle you face. You learn how to trust God beyond what you can see, feel, know, or even imagine. Especially when the unthinkable happens, then you have to trust God to provide something equally as unimaginable, something bigger than you can see from your current perspective.

Why would we be called overcomers if there was nothing to overcome? We would never be called more than conquerors if there were nothing to conquer, and if life never had any hurdles or challenges, faith would have no purpose. So, don't be dismayed when challenges come. The Word of God says his strength is made perfect in our weakness (see 2 Cor. 12:9) and our faith will be refined by the fire (see 1 Pet. 1:7).

The Enduring Faith of a Nation

When my oldest son, Joel, turned twenty-one, I made the impulsive decision that he and I should spend some time together in NYC. Our relationship was stretched by some of the pressures of a busy dad and a son entering into manhood and trying to find out who he was and what he was living for. We were already going to be in New Jersey as part of a Hillsong worship tour, and I made arrangements for Joel and me to stay in New York a few extra days and enjoy the city and attend some matches at the US Open tennis tournament—one of those items on my bucket list.

It was a great trip. We had an amazing night of worship in the New Jersey church, where the older pastor who was about to retire saw a prophecy come true. He had believed that before his time was over he would see their sanctuary full. And that night, not only was the sanctuary overcrowded, but the gym was also packed with people—and hundreds more were watching on a big screen outdoors. Late that night we were all still buzzing and decided to go into Manhattan for a bite to eat, so as tourists tend to do, we went into the heart of Times Square. A number of our team had never been to the United States before, let alone the Big Apple, so they were wide-eyed in wonder, as you can imagine.

We stood on Broadway and looked downtown to the World Trade Center towers standing magnificently taller than anything else in the distance. It was September 2001.

The next day the team went on to visit Lakewood Church in Houston, Texas, and Joel and I got "lost" in Manhattan for a couple of days. Sure enough, we attended the men's semifinal match at the US Open. As we watched from seats so high, we could see across the back of the stands to the majestic New York skyline several miles away and across the East River. That afternoon we chatted specifically about the wonder of those world-famous buildings, and I told Joel that a small plane once flew into the Empire State Building! We then started to speak about the atrocities of the Columbine school shooting in Colorado and the shooters' apparent plan to steal a small plane and fly it into the World Trade Center. So much tragedy in the world, and yet we were oblivious of what was just ahead.

We enjoyed the rest of the matches—Lleyton Hewitt, a fellow Aussie, had beaten Pete Sampras in the men's finals—and then flew on to Houston and then Atlanta. There, just two days later, Joel and I sat in our hotel room watching in disbelief as the unthinkable became reality. Horrific destruction unfolded in the heart of Manhattan and at the Pentagon. Our hearts were crushed, and our prayers joined with those of the many millions of other people around the country and the world.

The following week, with all flights grounded, we were effectively stuck in the United States, but there was no place I would rather have been. It was then that my love for America and its people took root at an even deeper level. It was then that I witnessed so many powerful moments of unity, sacrifice, and love that exemplify God's heart in the midst of chaos. So many Americans found ways to pull together and express their love for each other and support for their courageous country.

I'll never forget so many flags flying and the spirit of patriotism so evident everywhere. I'll never forget the generosity and hospitality of Pastor Jentezen Franklin and his wife, Cherise, our hosts in Georgia, who were stuck with over twenty Aussies unable to fly out to our next destination. It was a surreal feeling with no planes overhead and only a few businesses open.

Finally, we managed to hire a bus to get on with our tour, but it wasn't one of the tour buses that our music teams are accustomed to—built for musicians and bands to travel across states and between cities. No, it was a regular school bus with bench seats made for children, and certainly without any of the comforts of home. We spent seventeen hours on that bus through the night, attempting to sleep upright and eventually arriving in Saint Joseph, Missouri, ready for our next night of worship.

We had the privilege that weekend to be in Arizona for Sunday services at Phoenix First Assembly. Standing next to Pastor Tommy Barnett that day, I felt tears rolling down my cheeks as the congregation sang "America, America, God shed his grace on thee." I have never seen or felt such passion and patriotism as I felt in that service and throughout that week.

Joel and his family now live in lower Manhattan. He is copastor and part of the team in the Hillsong Church congregation we planted in New York City, only a few blocks from Ground Zero and the memorial there. Ironically, Joel's love for that great city was first stirred on our father-and-son trip in 2001. So much has changed in the United States and indeed the world since that terrible event, but my firsthand experience of the way the nation stood up and courageously stood together was a great collective example of robust, muscular, gutsy faith. Not military might but courage under fire—and that's what I believe we should strive for in our personal walk with our Father.

Terrible things happen sometimes—tsunamis and earthquakes, terrorist attacks and military conflicts, epidemics and disasters— but no matter how devastating those may be, we still have hope. And this hope we have is an anchor for our soul—alive and well, vibrant and dynamic, bringing joy to those who mourn and peace to those who struggle.

By faith we can subdue kingdoms, obtain promises, move mountains, and shut the mouths of lions. By faith we can enter God's will for our lives both here and in eternity. Pursue your God-given destiny with faith. Face insurmountable mountains and powerful "kings" with faith.

King David, who faced countless challenges, yet lived by faith, claimed at the end of his life: "I have been young, and now am old; yet I have not seen the righteous forsaken" (Ps. 37:25).

Shutting the Lion's Mouth

In order to strengthen your faith so that it becomes robust and muscular, so that it can open the door on God's glorious future, you must confront the enemy. Or, as it's described in Hebrews, "stop the mouths of lions" (see Heb. 6:22). This phrase refers to the story of Daniel in the lions' den, but it's no accident that we also find the devil compared to the same. "The devil roams about like a roaring lion, seeking whom he may devour" (see 1 Pet. 5:8). The enemy is out to consume us, to tempt us, and pull us away from God.

Whether you're literally shutting a lion's mouth, like Daniel, or engaging in spiritual warfare, both require a strong, muscular faith. Both require deliberate choices on your part as well. One of the best, most faith-building decisions you can make when it comes to the tempter is that he may not have a foothold in your life. What are the areas where the devil would like to devour your energies and drain you of your faith? Remember, he is a defeated foe and he's living on borrowed time. Sometimes we think he's out to take these enormous bites out of our lives, and sometimes he tries, but often I think it's the little nibbles each day that crumble our faith.

What is the enemy trying to steal from you to impede your relationship with God? How is the devil distracting you with a lot of roaring noise and big teeth? Where do you need to take a stand and shut the lion's mouth?

Sometimes I think we spend a lot of time fleeing from the devil, when we really need to stand our ground. The Bible doesn't teach us to flee from the devil; it teaches us to draw near to God, to resist the devil, so he will flee from you. We don't need to worry about running away from the devil and trying to hide from him. We simply need to focus on drawing near to God and his purpose for our lives. This is how we can best resist the devil. When he sees us drawing closer and closer to God, when he watches as our faith muscles grow bigger and stronger, he's forced to accept defeat.

The glorious future God has for you is far too important and too valuable to let the enemy steal it. The devil is nothing but a deceiver, and he goes around like a roaring lion, making a lot of noise and being scary. But sometimes when we run, we end up running right into the snares he's set for us. Someone told me that when you hear a lion roar in the jungle, it's not the greatest danger to you. Apparently, the male lions with their big manes and ferocious jaws will pick a spot and let out this tremendous roar. His prey will then run in the other direction where a female lion, old Leo's mate, is quietly waiting.

Sometimes it's not what we're running from that holds power over us; it's the act of running that pulls us away from God. We become focused on our own fear instead of standing strong in our faith and trusting God to help us overcome the enemy's traps. You've got to have the kind of muscular faith to stand up to the devil. How? By drawing near to God.

One of the greatest ways to draw near to God is through the power of worship. Worship is not just pretty songs. Worship is centered on who God is; it focuses on the greatness of God. When we sing, we magnify and glorify God and his character. If he's becoming bigger in our focus and in our hearts, then our problems don't have room to grow. The devil loses ground to plant his doubts and fears and snares. God gets the glory, and we've got the kind of strong, robust faith that can stare the devil down.

We don't live our lives scared of the devil because Jesus has given us the victory once and for all. We have Christ's promise of grace, forgiveness, and eternal life opening up a glorious future for our lives. We are no longer trapped by the sins of our past, the mistakes and pains our enemy tries to use to trip us. We can stare down his attempts at fear and intimidation, at his lies about who we are and who God is. We are children of the King and can claim our Father's promises. Like Joshua in the Promised Land, we still have to fight some battles, but the victory is already ours.

Your glorious future is secure!

CHAPTER SEVENTEEN

My Lord, My God

I love you Lord, I worship you
Hope which was lost, now stands renewed.
I give my life to honor this
The love of Christ, the Saviour King.

"Saviour King," Hillsong Music, 2007

Bobbie is probably the best skier in our family, but maybe that's because the rest of us snowboard—it's what us young people do. I may be the oldest and slowest snowboarder on the mountain, but our boys make up for my lack with their prowess. I initially took up snowboarding with the noble but naive intention of spending more quality time with them. However, after one particularly nasty spill ended in surgery for me, with plates and pins inserted in my elbow, it became clear that maybe there were easier ways to spend rewarding family time with my adult sons. However, I did achieve one thing for the family through my snowboarding endeavors: My escapades have been the target of hours of family tales, accompanied by great mirth and laughter around the Houston dinner table—not quite what I had in mind.

On one occasion, our boys lured Bobbie and me up the ski lift to a particularly high mountain peak. As we alighted the mountaintop, Bobbie was clearly unsure, but our sons can be very persuasive, and we united in our commitment to whatever lay ahead of us. We set out together, but after heading several hundred meters down a relatively easy early slope, everything began to change. The black diamonds on the marker sign were insight into the perilous path ahead.

It was already too late to make our way back to the lift, so there was no real choice but to continue stoically toward the uncertainty that awaited us. It was not long before we were standing on the edge of a virtual cliff with a breathtaking sheer drop. This provided no real challenge for the boys, who were beyond it in a moment and had disappeared through the tree line, as was normally the way. Somehow, I also miraculously managed to traverse my way down, negotiating the dangers and making my way to safer ground.

Unfortunately, for Bobbie, chivalry was not really the order of the day. Instead, she was left on the edge of the cliff to fend for herself, while all the men in her life were long gone. She found herself literally pinned to the wall of this snow-covered mountain, knowing that she had nowhere to go but down! Seeing her hesitation and understanding her fear, a kind gentleman stopped alongside her, took a look at the cliff, and said, "Ma'am, you've just got to commit to the mountain."

So that was exactly what she did. Ultimately my brave wife made her way back to the base healthy and intact, with a story to tell.

Sometimes, when you feel cornered by life, hemmed in by less than ideal circumstances, you have to do the same thing and commit to the mountain. You have to take that leap of faith, trusting that God will guide you and lead you through the trials and temptations you're facing. So many times in life are like trying to ski over the edge of a steep precipice when you can't see a path down. There's no way to turn back and no way to go forward. You feel stuck and afraid, at a loss for hope. These are the times when you must exercise your faith like never before, stepping into the glorious future God has for you even though you can't see what's ahead. There are times in life when you just have to commit to your mountain.

Doubts and Disappointments

Following Jesus on the grand adventure of a faith-filled life requires risk taking. Keeping your eyes on him while he calls you out upon the water, into the great unknown where feet may fail just like Peter, is never easy. Fears and doubts assault you and shout all the reasons why you can't or shouldn't do what God calls you to do. As frightening as it may feel at times, you must be willing to keep moving, being faithful in the small things as you ask God for the strength, courage, and resources to take the next step.

These dark moments in life when the uncertainty of the future terrifies you require a deeper, grittier kind of faith. These are the times when God asks you not only to trust him but also to surrender all areas of your life to him. We often assume automatically that knowing God is the same as making him Lord of our lives. But I'm convinced, especially when facing the crossroads and crucibles of life, we must surrender to God as our Lord. Nothing can open up the doorway to your glorious future like experiencing a personal revelation of Jesus' Lordship over your life.

We see this kind of revelation in one particular disciple of

Jesus, a man who wanted to believe but needed concrete proof to bolster his faith—Thomas. Notice the cause for Thomas' doubts and how they lead him to his special, very unique revelation with the risen Christ.

> Now Thomas, called the Twin, one of the twelve, was not with them when Jesus came. The other disciples therefore said to him, "We have seen the Lord."
>
> So he said to them, "Unless I see in His hands the print of the nails, and put my finger into the print of the nails, and put my hand into His side, I will not believe."
>
> And after eight days His disciples were again inside, and Thomas with them. Jesus came, the doors being shut, and stood in the midst, and said, "Peace to you!" Then He said to Thomas, "Reach your finger here, and look at My hands; and reach your hand here, and put it into My side. Do not be unbelieving, but believing."
>
> And Thomas answered and said to Him, "My Lord and my God!"
>
> Jesus said to him, "Thomas, because you have seen Me, you have believed. Blessed are those who have not seen and yet have believed." (John 20:24–29)

As Thomas discovered, life has its disappointments, and if ever the Lordship of Jesus Christ will be tested in our lives it's when we are in the face of disappointment. It's an interesting word, *disappointment*. With the prefix *dis-*, meaning "to go in the opposite direction," added to *appointment*, this word captures that feeling of having missed something that we think should have happened. Or perhaps even a circumstance that took you off course from your God-given appointment. A failed appointment. A missed appointment.

But God doesn't disappoint us—our own limited perceptions and expectations disappoint us. No, he is not the one who disappoints us, but instead he appoints us to a glorious future. He's got an appointed plan for your life, a purpose for your time here on earth. However, sometimes the gap between our personal disappointment and our God-given appointment can be long, and it's in this gap that we see Thomas' relationship with Jesus tested. As a follower of Christ, he had heard his Master speak all those words we know about and likely some we don't. He had witnessed miracles and healings, transformations and life-changing encounters. And then suddenly, everything seemed to go downhill—high-powered persecutors, Jesus' arrest, his crucifixion, and his burial. It must have seemed like a beautiful dream that suddenly evaporated in the harsh light of day.

So now there's a rumor circulating that Christ's body is not in the tomb, that he has in fact risen from the dead. But Thomas, like the other disciples, must have felt suspended in the gap between human disappointment and divine appointment. And there's nothing like disappointment and disorientation to reveal how firmly connected we are to Christ's Lordship, God's appointment, and surrendering every part of our life to him.

Love and Liberation

Lordship sometimes gets lost when vulnerability closes in on you. So before we judge this disciple and forever label him "Doubting Thomas," I think we can all honestly appreciate his desire to have proof, certainty, and stability restored in his life. The disciples were feeling incredibly vulnerable. It was nighttime, and the darkness mirrored their own confusion and uncertainty. They felt exposed and unprotected, so they retreated to this little room upstairs in a place they assumed to be safe. Nonetheless, they locked the doors and began to discuss their situation and what some of them had witnessed.

Then suddenly Jesus came and stood in their midst and said to them, "Peace be with you"—even though the doors were locked! This is what fear does to us, locking us up inside ourselves, afraid to engage in the world and continue on the path on which God placed us. We look for a refuge, put the walls up, pull the blinds down, and lock ourselves away, hoping the storm will pass or we'll figure out some solution to our problems. The future feels threatening to us, not glorious, because we can't imagine how to get through the present pain inside us and the turmoil boiling over around us.

Just as Jesus showed up inside the disciples' locked room and wished them peace, we also know he brings this peace to all of us. I love that Jesus would not only recognize the disciples' doubts and fears, but choose to show up in the midst of them. God often shows up and surprises us with something that seems impossible. Thomas wanted Jesus to let him feel the nails in Jesus' hands and touch his hand to Jesus' side. If he could experience this kind of certainty, and only then, he would be willing to believe that Jesus was truly alive again.

So Jesus gave him what he asked for, singling Thomas out from the group so that he could experience up close and personal the very evidence he had so skeptically demanded. I can imagine the kind smile on his face as he beckoned Thomas forward, understanding his humanity in that moment and feeling compassion toward his friend and the unknown circumstances he was facing.

But Thomas didn't have to put his finger through the nail holes in Jesus' palms or touch the scar in his side. He immediately said, "My Lord and my God!" We're not told this, but somehow I imagine Thomas falling on his knees there at the feet of Jesus, probably feeling a flood of mixed emotions: shame for not believing, joy at realizing his Master was alive, and excitement about the implications of his personal revelation of the risen Christ.

It's worth noting, too, the way Thomas proclaimed Jesus as both Lord and God. It was not just an admission that yes, only the Son of God could have risen from the grave, but a complete and total surrendering to this God. So it's a powerful thing when he's able to say, "My Lord and my God," because he had had a revelation of Jesus like he had never had before that moment. Doubting Thomas became declaring Thomas. His doubt and disappointment transformed into God's anointing and appointing. All of a sudden, instead of having a mind filled with doubt he had a heart filled with trust and could declare, "My Lord and my God!"

Personal Lordship can be a challenge to grasp and to apply to your life because it's so big and comprehensive. It's easy to think of him as the Lord of creation or the Lord of salvation. We can accept that he's Lord over Heaven and earth, eternal and limitless. But when we apply his Lordship to our daily lives, it suddenly costs us something. We can no longer live the same way we once did, doubting and wondering, feeling afraid and stuck in place. Lordship liberates us to live fully, to relate personally, and to take the next step in our journey with Christ.

Applying his Lordship to all areas can indeed be scary and challenging. Yes, he's Lord of your life now, but does that have to include everything? What about Lord of your finance? What about Lord of your relationships? What about Lord when you're dating? What about Lord of your sexuality? What about Lord of your priorities? What about Lord of your career? What about Lord of the way you act with your boss and coworkers? What about Lord in all other parts of your life? Only when we fully surrender all that we are, all that we have, and all that we hope can we truly, genuinely, understand the love and liberation that comes from having Jesus as Lord.

Comparisons and Convictions

Personal revelations of the living Christ cannot be contrived or manufactured. I believe if we sincerely seek God and draw near to him, then he draws near to us, as we're told in the book of James. But sometimes in life when we are going through a rough patch, we can feel like everyone else is handling their lives in a more Christlike manner than we are. Others seem to be getting closer with God, growing in their faith, and on fire with the power of the Holy Spirit fueling their big, spacious lives.

Sometimes we pastors and leaders, who should know better, can be tempted to compare our ministry momentum with others around the world. You know, we see the way God is blessing others in their ministry and increasing their influence for his kingdom, and we wonder why we haven't experienced that kind of favor yet. Perhaps we do not begrudge our friends and partners in ministry, but we can often stand back and wonder when our time will come to experience our own unique revelation of God's power in our midst. Like a jealous child watching their dad reward a sibling, people sometimes wonder if they're missing out on what everyone else seems to be enjoying. It is in those moments that we must remain faithful and just keep doing what God has called us to do.

One of the things I can honestly tell you about Bobbie and myself: We have always tried to live our lives authentically and commit to the principles we teach others in our own marriage and in our lives together, no matter what's happening around us. Certainly, we've made some mistakes along the way, but from the earliest days of our marriage, we made a commitment to put God first in our finances, our relationships, our words, our actions, our leadership—everything. Not having much at the time we made those commitments, we didn't realize the tension that putting God first can cause at times. But I love the fact that I can stand today as a pastor and look everyone in the eye, from first-time visitors to inquisitive journalists to longtime friends and family, and say that everything we teach at Hillsong Church we have endeavored to live out in our own lives.

When my son Ben was seventeen or eighteen, he was finishing high school, or "Year Twelve," as we call it here in Australia. While other countries have spring break as a traditional time for young people to celebrate, party, and vacation together, we have what's called "schoolies." Just like spring break, this season can strike fear in the heart of so many parents. Many kids go wild and get into all kinds of trouble during schoolies week—some harmless enough, but in many cases excessive, dangerous, and even deadly.

Our Ben was like any other teenager in that season of his life. He loved the Lord, along with his family and his friends; he loved Wildlife, our high school youth ministry, along with the other pursuits I've mentioned, such as wakeboarding and surfing. He also loved his school friends and unchurched mates, and even at a maturing age, his pastoral heart and deep care for people was very evident. But he was also young and impressionable and clearly feeling pulled by his friends into un-Christlike things that represented different standards than the ones Bobbie and I had prayed for and believed for all our kids. So in this season, when his final exams were over and as the end of his high school years approached, tragedy struck.

Ben went with his friends to a high school party one summer night and had agreed to be the designated driver—driving my car, by the way, which will always increase a parent's prayer life. The party was an end-of-school celebration, and dozens of young people were in attendance. Later that night, as they were leaving the party, Ben and his mates came out of the house, no doubt making a lot of noise as teenagers do, with plenty of bravado while making their way to the car. The party was over and had spilled out onto the road, when conversation turned to squabbling over who would sit where.

Suddenly, out of nowhere, a car with no headlights appeared. As I understand it, without slowing at all, the car careened in the direction of the partygoers and ran straight into one of the boys Ben was with, throwing him through the air and slamming him into the curb. His head gushed from the impact. Miraculously, he survived, but he suffered terrible head injuries with serious ongoing consequences, not the kind of thing you would ever wish anyone to experience or witness. It was a horrible reality for everyone involved, and it hit Ben especially hard, resulting in recurring nightmares.

Somehow, by the grace of God, this accident became a catalyst for Ben to think deeply about his life and reconsider his current priorities.

With all of these things weighing heavily within him, and facing a somewhat daunting season of transition from high school to the future unknown, Ben made the decision to attend summer camp with our youth group just a few weeks later. Like so many kids, that year at camp Ben had his own personal revelation of Jesus, a life-defining, literally life-transforming experience.

It's what every parent hopes for when they send their kids off to church camp—and it's why, to this day, we love offering and supporting these summer camps for young people. Mixed in with "tribal wars" and crazy adventures, young people often encounter God in a radical way; camp ignites a fire within them that changes many of these kids forever and launches them into the glorious future that God has prepared for them.

Complete Surrender

Like Thomas, Ben had an encounter that left him proclaiming, "My Lord and my God!" and the fruit of that revelation was immediately apparent as the near impossible started to happen. Ben loved sports, and he was good at them—and he was good at anything you stand on sideways. So whether it was a wakeboard, a surfboard, a snowboard, or a skateboard, generally he was up for it, and he totally loved it. But when he returned from camp, Ben explained to us that he felt in his heart that he should lay down all of those pursuits for twelve months. And that was exactly what he did! That's how a parent knows there really must be a God!

Ben put aside all his favorite activities and sport hobbies for that year. He didn't go surfing or skating but instead read through his Bible in a calendar year, then decided to study ministry and leadership at Hillsong International Leadership College. A short time later, we agreed it would be a great experience for him to travel for twelve months and spend time interning at Hillsong Kiev, Hillsong London, and then with friends in Virginia Beach on the East Coast of the United States. It was a challenging year in many ways, away from everything and everyone he loved, including his pretty young girlfriend, Lucille. But Ben came back a changed young man, and we were amazed and so grateful.

Our son had experienced a personal revelation of God that opened his eyes to his glorious future, one we are beginning to see played out even now—and it is better than we could ever have dreamed. Of course today, Ben and Lucille and their three beautiful young daughters are living in Los Angeles, pioneering and leading Hillsong LA. However, it was in those days as a teenager when, like Thomas, Ben confessed, "My Lord and my God," and his life got into the slipstream of the glorious future God had prepared for him. When we all watched God turn disappointment into God-appointment.

I pray that you can have this kind of Thomas-Lordship revelation in your own life, an encounter where you not only know Jesus as the Son of God, your Savior, but one where you surrender yourself to him as your Lord. It won't be easy at times because it requires ongoing, complete surrender. You will have to be brutally honest about areas you've been protecting and hiding, secrets that have been locked away and covered over.

If you want to follow Jesus and experience the fullness of a life in which you live, love, and lead as he did, then you must let go of everything. It's time to unlock your closed doors and open the shutters. Drink in the lessons of disappointment and allow the restorative rain of God-given appointment to bring hope to your heart. Lower the walls on those areas of your life where you've been afraid to allow Jesus to be Lord, and let him in to your hurt, doubt, and fears for the future.

Just as Bobbie had to do while skiing, you must commit to the mountain and take the next step, trusting God with every ounce of your being, knowing he is your loving Father and has your very best interests at heart. Don't just recognize that he is an all-powerful, all-knowing God, but embrace the personal encounters you've had with him over the years. If you haven't had that personal revelation of the living Jesus yet, then ask God to bring you to that place of surrender and trust. He is always faithful to keep his promises, and like Thomas, you will go from "I can't believe" to "My Lord and my God!"

CHAPTER EIGHTEEN

Hand and Heart

**Lord I give you my heart, I give you my soul.
I live for you alone.
Every breath that I take, every moment I'm awake.
Lord, have your way in me.**
"I Give You My Heart," Hillsong Music, 1996

There are more than seven billion people on the earth today, and I would dare to guess that a good majority of them have at least heard the name Bono. One of the most influential musicians and poets of our generation, his distinct sound and musicianship has taken the world by storm. His band, U2, the Irish musical phenomenon, is considered one of the most politically and environmentally active bands of this era, and their sounds and songs fill stadiums to sold-out tours, year after year. Bono is their recognizable, low-key front man. He is incredibly gifted, and when he writes, sings, and performs, he is so clearly doing what he was created to do. When he stands on a stage at a crowded concert, he is fulfilling his calling, as he maximizes his gifts and utilizes his talents.

Yet Bono has so obviously lived with far weightier things encompassing his heart. His passion for the poor and underprivileged, for injustice and political integrity—for the desperate lack in many countries of the world—has set him apart from other entertainers.

Today, Bono's influence has positioned him at the table among the world's most powerful kings and presidents, and he lends his influence to the cause of ending world poverty, to the desperate and the uneducated in this generation's most needy nations.

Some may point out that his music is secular and indeed it is, but he himself is a man of strong faith doing what God has gifted him to do. He has used what is in his hand—musicianship and his calling outworked through his gift and talents—to fulfill what's in his heart, his destiny, and purpose.

In an earlier chapter we discussed 2 Timothy 1:9—you are saved, called, and graced *for purpose*. It's *all* about his purpose. Your gifts and talents, time and energy, life and health, finances and resources, your marriage and family, and your priorities and focus are all about purpose. Not only is it all about his specific and personalized purpose for you, but about his collective purpose for all of creation.

Ecclesiastes 3:11 in the Amplified Bible says: "He has made everything beautiful in its time. He also has planted eternity in men's hearts and minds [a divinely implanted sense of a purpose working through the ages which nothing under the sun but God alone can satisfy]."

You were created, gifted, and graced for God's eternal purpose, a divinely implanted purpose. So, what's yours?

Lost and Found

Just as we discussed in Part 1, A Big Life, God gives each of us unique gifts and vocations along with the grace to fulfill them. Invariably at some point in life, though, most of us will struggle to understand our calling and our distinctive purpose.

I don't know about you, but there have been times when I've tried to be something I'm not, and it always got me into trouble. For example, a few years ago, the night before Hillsong Conference was about to begin, I was standing in front of my bathroom mirror with my hair clipper and thought I would have a go at being my own hairdresser. Needless to say, after trimming my facial stubble, I forgot to attach the comb and cut a track into my hair, similar to the impact of a mower on an overgrown lawn. I ended up completely bald, much to the amusement of thousands who gathered on the first night of Hillsong Conference... *not* my best look!

A couple of times I've had someone who really excelled in their profession become a Christian and join our family at Hillsong. Subsequently, they will then ask me what it is that God wants them to do. One such person was an award-winning professional athlete, an international celebrity known for his strong character both on and off the playing field. A well-intentioned (but I believe, misguided) Christian had suggested that he should quit sports and give away all his money, in order to "serve God." When he asked me what God wanted him to do with his life, he was genuinely considering retiring from the playing field and attending Bible college, even though he was at the peak of his ability and career.

I saw things very differently! It was and is my belief that he is serving God by doing what God has gifted him to do. He has been graced with a freakish ability and by using what's in his hand—in this case, a football—he has a platform to live out his vibrant faith at a level of influence that many others could only wish for! He didn't need to make a radical change in order to align his calling with his purpose. God had obviously created him to be a gifted athlete and blessed him with opportunities that he had maximized for his success. He seemed relieved to learn that there was so much he could do for the kingdom by simply continuing to be where God had placed him.

Similarly, my friend John pastored a church in a small town in England, and a well-known billionaire named Bob attended his church. I have a memory of Bob playing bass guitar in one of their services. He and John had become good friends. John once told me, with a mischievous smile on his face, how one day Bob the Billionaire came to him with tears in his eyes and said, "John, I would give anything to do what you do." And John the Pastor humorously recalled how he looked straight back at him with tears in his eyes and said, "Bob, I would give anything to do what you do!"

It was a lighthearted conversation I had with John, but I think the point is very poignant: to spend your life wishing you were somebody else is to live frustrated and discouraged, and you won't be able to build much from that posture. Some people are graced to build a business, others to write music, others to lead people, and so on. I am graced to be a leader (not a hairdresser), and still others are called to be professional athletes. God doesn't make mistakes. He knew exactly what he was doing and was very intentional when he made you and me. Stay within your grace, live there, and encourage others to do the same. It is then that you will find a satisfaction and sense of purpose in your everyday calling.

You don't have to quit being who you are just because you've surrendered your life to Christ. When you follow Jesus on your adventure of faith and experience a big, spacious life, you will become more of who you were meant to be, not less. In fact, it's rather ironic that in order to be more of who God made us to be we simply need to quit trying to be anything else. "He who finds his life will lose it, and he who loses his life for My sake will find it" (Matt. 10:39).

Losing your life for the sake of following Christ does not mean losing your gifts and talents. I'm convinced we don't have the right to lay down something that is a true gift from God. Certainly we may have talents and abilities we've put to poor use—such as putting a gift for business to an illegal enterprise or using a gift of the imagination to deceptive ends. These may indeed need to be relinquished so that God can refine and restore the foundational gifts he placed in you. But all too often, I suspect we underestimate what God can use.

The American writer Frederick Buechner explains, "The place God calls you to is the place where your deep gladness and the world's deep hunger meet."

Did you know the word *calling* literally means "to shout aloud"? Some people are waiting for a whisper from heaven to direct their path, when the opportunity before them is shouting loudly.

The same is true for you. Your calling may be blaring like a siren in your ear, sounding an alarm that's been going off for some time. What are you good at? What seems to come naturally to you? What opportunity lies right in front of you? Are you artistic? Love numbers and balanced order? Enjoy working with your hands in the garden? Have a passion for music? Feel at home in the classroom? Often you may be waiting for some still, small voice to whisper in your ear, when your calling is blasting out loud all around you!

Master Craftsman

Talk about sports leaves some people cold, but as you've probably gathered by now, I love almost every kind of sport! Growing up in New Zealand, I shared many a young boy's dream of playing for the famed All Black Rugby Team. The All Blacks have enjoyed enormous success through the years as New Zealand's national team, whose name is derived from the all-black gear in which they play. However, anyone who has seen my gangly walking style and apparent "gift" for clumsiness would know that the chances I had to be a future professional rugby star were slim to zero (at best). I smile when I think about it, because I am very comfortable with the knowledge that God made me with a different set of gifts, abilities, interests, and resources in order to fulfill the calling he had placed on my life.

Growing up I was never voted "most likely to succeed," and I was never really chosen for any leadership roles at school or even in our youth group or church. But as a teenager, I had a burning passion to serve God. Remarkably, as the opportunity finally came my way to lead a Thursday night Bible study and a house meeting in the youth ministry of a small church in South Auckland, something just clicked. I was fresh out of Bible college, green, and lacking any real firsthand experience, but I trusted that God saw in me the skills that the job required. I relied on him to draw out of me the natural interest and concern I have for people, and to couple that with my love for him and my commitment to his Church.

Instinctively I knew to gather the right leaders around me, and soon my little Bible study began to grow and grow until it outgrew the lounge room, and young people were spilling into the hallway and out the door. After a few months, the house was far too small to contain all of the spiritually zealous young people who wanted to squeeze in. Many of these kids had no background of faith in Jesus—but as young people brought their friends and the Holy Spirit drew their hearts toward God, something very powerful began to happen.

Clearly I was always going to be a misfit on the football field, but I found serving and growing a church something that seemed quite natural. As long as I focused on what I could do and not on what I might like to do but couldn't, I discovered a new sense of alignment in my life. I developed an awareness that my gifting, calling, and purpose all fit together as if designed by a master craftsman, which they were.

My experience is not unique. We are all called to live out our salvation with confidence and a sense of peace that comes when our lives are aligned with our divine purpose. Paul explains it this way: "For God has not given us a spirit of fear, but of power and of love and of a sound mind. Therefore do not be ashamed of the testimony of our Lord, nor of me His prisoner, but share with me in the sufferings for the gospel according to the power of God, who has saved us and called us with a holy calling, not according to our works, but according to His own purpose and grace which was given to us in Christ Jesus before time began" (2 Tim. 1:7–9).

Regardless of where you may be in your life right now, God has brought you to this moment for his purposes. Despite whatever mistakes you've made or regrets you may harbor, he has graced you for a glorious future. He can turn your errors into life lessons that can help others. He can transform your pain into compassion to heal those around you. He can utilize the humblest abilities and the most developed expertise for his glory. You simply have to be willing to follow in Jesus' footsteps as you look ahead at where God wants to lead you.

Hot Rod

As I travel around the world, I'm amazed at the similarities among vastly different people. Some are young adults just starting out in life, and others are middle-aged and redefining themselves and what they want their lives to be. Still others are advanced in age and wondering if it's too late to fulfill that little tickle in their soul, that ache in their heart that God instilled in them for his purposes. Many of them ask me, "Brian, how do I go about making my dreams come true? How do I know if my dreams are God's purpose for my life?"

While there's no one-answer-fits-all response, I usually tell them the same thing: Use what's in your hand! This is the response God gave Moses after choosing him to lead the people of Israel out of slavery in Egypt. You may recall that God appears as a burning bush to Moses, telling him that he must try to negotiate with Pharaoh and secure a peaceful release for the Hebrew captives. Yet Moses responds the way many of us do: "Who am I that I should go to Pharaoh, and that I should bring the children of Israel out of Egypt?" (Exod. 3:11).

So God tells Moses to explain to Pharaoh and the Egyptians that Moses serves as God's spokesman, empowered as a divine ambassador to secure his people's freedom. Moses isn't buying it and keeps thinking ahead: "But suppose they will not believe me or listen to my voice; suppose they say, 'The LORD has not appeared to you'" (Exod. 4:1). That's when God gets very concrete and direct, answering in the form of a question: "What is that in your hand?" (Exod. 4:2).

I felt God speak exactly those same words to me in the early years of Hillsong Church. I remember looking around and wondering where we would ever find the worship team, the small group leaders, a youth pastor, and children's workers. But as I considered the options amid the small crew that had gathered, I felt the words God spoke to Moses echo in my spirit. "What's that in your hand?"

Over thirty years later, we continue to staff and lead our church with the people whom God has placed in our hands: those who have proven themselves within the life of the church, whose heart for God and his House have been their greatest qualifications. We don't "hire" people who have no understanding or empathy with the DNA of our church, and this is evidenced in a wonderful team of sacrificial staff and leaders who are remarkably gifted.

The blessing we've enjoyed and the influence we have been granted through Hillsong worship has never been built on hiring the best of the best, or scooping up those who are serving in other churches, or capitalizing on those who are building their own worship platform. We have simply trusted God and worked with the people he has placed in our hands, and then watched as he uses ordinary people to do extraordinary things.

Similarly to Moses, when he recognized the power of the regular shepherd's staff in his hand, it quickly becomes a serpent right before his very eyes. When God instructs Moses to pick it up by its tail, it becomes a rod again. Moses knew this trick was sure to get Pharaoh's attention—and it did!

We often respond to God's calling on our lives just like Moses, making excuses and claiming—often sincerely—that we don't have what we need to do the job. How can we actualize the dream God has for our glorious future if we don't have the resources, the degree, the property, the capital, or the supporters? All I can say is that we have a perspective limited by what we see on earth, which keeps us from recognizing the invisible, unlimited resources of our Father in Heaven. Also, as I've discovered, what I think I need to get the job done and what God thinks I need are not always the same thing. Like Jesus blessing the little boy's two fish and five loaves into enough fish sandwiches to feed over five thousand people, God can do a lot with a little. His blessings are designed to multiply and create a domino effect of positive impact.

Unlock Your Future

Whether you recognize it or not, the seeds for your glorious future have already been sown. Your various life experiences, relationships, even your mistakes have all contributed to fertilize those seeds of purpose. The challenge for most people, however, is closing the gap between what's in their hand and what's in their heart. It feels like an insurmountable distance between the cubicle and the corner office, between painting walls and painting portraits, between writing ad copy and signing copies of your best seller. But often the distance isn't as great as it appears. And often God's route to your glorious future relies on his unique sense of direction, not the logical, straightforward route you might envision.

So don't overlook what feels familiar and even tedious. You are already an expert in a number of fields and methods, whether you realize it or not. Channel your frustration working the fast-food counter into new and better methods of customer service. Consider the limitations of your favorite social media source and improve upon them. Identify what you enjoy most about managing your team and see if you can specialize in it. Take joy and satisfaction in the efficient running of your household and be generous with the resources you have. There are numerous ways to transform the staff or stick in your hand into a lightning rod of God's power and purpose.

Unfortunately, often when we try to align our calling with our purpose, a sense of entitlement creeps in. We become fixated on the higher prize at the expense of our current talents. However, God's Word is consistent on the principle of stewardship: "He who is faithful in what is least is faithful also in much" (Luke 16:10). If you're not willing to start small and grow from what you've been given, then you will likely remain frustrated. Your vision of a global organization starts at the grassroots level first. Your international business venture begins with how you conduct your self-employed start-up. Your loving, cohesive family begins with small decisions to be home early to eat meals together. You can't expect to be at the top of your game and get the outcomes you long for if you don't put in the work.

God wants you to fully engage with the resources and gifts that he's entrusted to you. He wants you investing them and producing a greater return for his kingdom, not burying them or using them for your own purposes. One of the main reasons we've continued to explore new frontiers of ministry, like planting churches in "graveyard" cities or changing the plight of hurting people in desperate situations and desperate places, is so that we can multiply the return on God's investment. He has been so generous and bountiful in his many blessings on Hillsong

Church. These are given out of his love as our Father and as a reflection of his glory. He doesn't give us opportunities just so we can build a bigger building or have another conference; he gives us opportunities so we can love others as he loves us. In fact, the vision statement of Hillsong Church since its inception remains the same today: "To reach and influence the world by building a large Christ-centered, Bible-based church, changing mindsets and empowering people to lead and impact in every sphere of life." We are all about equipping people to prosper in their sphere of life, and empowering them to use what's in their hand to lead, have an impact, and fulfill what's in their hearts.

Now is the time to close the gap between where you are in the present and where God is calling you to go in the future. The doorway to your glorious future is likely to be open already, waiting for you to push and walk through it. If you're frustrated by unrealized dreams and ongoing disappointments, ask God to reveal your next steps. Ask him to transform the rod in your hand into the key to unlock your future. Don't try to jump too far too soon; instead just ask God to show you today's step, the one priority to keep you moving forward.

> Trust in the LORD, and do good;
> dwell in the land, and feed on His faithfulness.
> Delight yourself also in the LORD,
> and He shall give you the desires of your heart.
> (Psalm 37:3–4)

What is in your hand and on your heart is the key to your glorious future!

CHAPTER NINETEEN

Don't Stop

I'll look to the cross as my failure is lost,
In the light of Your glorious grace.
Let the ruins come to life, in the beauty of Your
Name
Rising up from the ashes, God forever You reign.
"Glorious Ruins," Hillsong Music, 2013

I consider myself a seasoned traveler, and I pride myself in my ability to negotiate airport terminals, security lines, and immigration booths quicker than any other traveler I've encountered. (I think Bobbie would probably find a way to use the word *impatient* here.) Impatient or not, I see airport escalators and moving walkways as an experienced traveler's best friend—with every step, you go twice the distance in half the time! So I can never understand why some people still stop and let the walkway do all the work, especially when they are lost in conversation and seemingly oblivious to the fact that they are blocking the path of people like myself—on a mission to commute from terminal to terminal with a blinkered sense of purpose and intent.

For instance, I was in the Dubai airport a few years ago, connecting to another flight, and I was simply amazed by some of the world's longest escalators and moving walkways. They seemed to stretch for miles, crisscrossing several stories, their gleaming, polished chrome making it all look like a city from another planet. Thousands of people rushed and hustled to their flights, most looking vague and with little idea of where they were going and how they were going to get there.

I found myself riding on an escalator with hundreds of people ahead of me, when I suddenly heard a serious commotion happening up ahead. A petite-framed lady wearing a burka was approaching the end of the escalator clearly in a panic, unsure how to transition back to the stationary floor. Apparently, she had never seen a moving walkway before and she wasn't sure how she was meant to step off. So as the escalator came to an end, she took a tiny step onto firm ground and just stopped in her tracks. The problem was, everybody behind her still had momentum and nowhere to go—creating a domino effect. Luggage, purses, children, and passengers sprawled everywhere as they were unable to halt their continuing forward motion. The walkway had ended, but the lady wasn't supposed to stop.

And therein lies the moral to this story. When something's over, don't stop. The end of an era is not the completion of a destiny.

Unplanned but Not Unknown

There are times in our life when our momentum comes to an abrupt end. A season ends and catches us by surprise, and we're left wondering how to take the next step like the woman in the airport. It could be losing a job or being forced to switch careers. It could be a promotion or a new position of leadership. It might be a new relationship, or the end of one, as someone moves away or goes a different direction. It could be the completion of a goal, getting a degree or moving to the home you've always wanted, or the last of your children leaving for college. Whatever it is, you're left feeling a bit disoriented and uncertain, afraid to take the next step or unsure of the direction in which to make your next move.

But just because something's over doesn't mean you should stop. Whether you're reaching a milestone or facing an unexpected loss, you may not know how to go on, but you have to trust that as long as you have life and breath, God has a plan for your next step. On the path of faith the journey takes us to places we never dreamed, some more beautiful and joyous than anything we could hope for, others more dark and disappointing than we've ever faced. But following Jesus means we keep going even when we don't know how or even exactly where. Jesus' own earthly father, Joseph, experienced exactly this.

As I've done for thirty-two consecutive Christmases, I sat down this Christmas to prepare a message for the people of our church. These days, my Christmas message is preached live at our Hills Campus and sent simultaneously to over forty different services in nineteen different locations, and through technology it is streamed around the world. This year, in preparation, I found myself meditating on Joseph.

Joseph, several months before Jesus' birth, was about to enter into his greatest victory to date. His family and Mary's had agreed upon a contract, and they were betrothed to be married. He was promised to a beautiful girl from a perfect family, with ancestry all the way back to Israel's royal household and King David himself. Both Joseph and Mary had shown their affection and approval for each other by drinking two cups of wine in a culturally traditional ceremony, and Joseph had taken his leave in order to prepare for his bride-to-be.

Matthew 1:18–23 documents the moment that Joseph found out the woman he was betrothed to, but had not yet been intimate with, was pregnant. The words that stood out to me in verse 18 were the words *after* and *before*. What a dream destroyer for him: "*after* Mary was betrothed but *before* they came together." No doubt Joseph had looked forward to being married to Mary. Just as many of us do, he had allowed himself to dream of the children they would have and what those moments would entail. He imagined the joy of holding his firstborn, family gathered around in celebration—and now this. He didn't even know who the father was; he just knew it wasn't him.

It was the most inconvenient shock and it came at the most inconvenient time. He was betrothed, a contract that could only be annulled by divorce; they were fully committed but had not yet moved into their glorious future. It was in these moments before the Holy Spirit had spoken to Joseph that he must have felt so alone, so empty, and so uncertain of what was to come. Yet what seemed like the end for Joseph was only just the beginning. His current circumstance may have been unplanned, but to God, it was not unknown.

Battleground

If you're currently in transition, facing the end of something, perhaps the beginning of something else, you must look at this crossroads as a battlefront. You know how historic sites often have markers describing important battles that took place on the grounds? "Here was the Battle of Gallipoli"—the battle that marked the first major military operation for our ANZACs (the Australian and New Zealand Army Corps): This fierce and heroically fought battle on Turkish soil is generally seen as the marker for the birth of national consciousness in our part of the world. Conversely the English would find, "Here was the Battle of Hastings," and you would find "Here was the Battle of Gettysburg" if you live in the States.

When we face the end of one chapter of our lives and before we begin the next, it's often the catalyst for a battle. You see, our enemy the devil often tries to wedge a foot in the door and catch us off guard during these times of transition. He's hoping we'll feel disoriented and uncertain, afraid and a bit wary. He would love to derail your journey of faith and send you down a wrong path, deceiving you into thinking you'd reached a dead end.

In other words, the devil would love to seize your growth opportunities from you and turn you into a nonproductive, joyless individual. He can't rob you of your salvation, but he can certainly try to undermine your purpose and satisfaction. Satan would love to be the end of your spiritual adventure, the impenetrable roadblock separating you from God. But he can't do it. God's bigger and more powerful. Whenever we feel like we've reached the end and can't keep going, it's simply a temporary illusion the devil's trying to maintain.

As challenging as it may be, if you want to live a life with ongoing momentum, a life that's big and full and bursting with joy and meaning, then you need to see God in the end of things as well as the beginning. Because if we trust God with the end of things, he will fulfill his good purpose in our lives.

I love the fact that it ain't over until God says it's over. Just because you lose something precious to you, just because a chapter ended abruptly and unexpectedly, it doesn't mean your life is over. And it certainly doesn't mean that God has forgotten you or abandoned you for one moment. As difficult as it may be to see sometimes—when you've lost a loved one or lost your job or received devastating news—the best is yet to come. Just like with Joseph, God's glorious future is about to be revealed!

Confident and Steadfast

Pastoring a church, and particularly a large church, it's inevitable that you will have opportunity to "rejoice with those who rejoice, and weep with those who weep"—and often at the same time. As a young couple is rejoicing in the safe arrival of their miracle baby, perhaps another family may be grieving over a sudden loss, or a young person may be heartbroken by a fractured relationship. It's the seasons of life.

I recall how Jay, a young and gifted key member of our staff, faced something so painful just a few years ago. His father, Gary, who was a little younger than me, was fit and healthy and loved to swim and surf on the Central Coast, the beach-lined region just north of Sydney where they lived. On that day he came out of the surf, grabbed his chest, and fell to the ground, dying of a heart attack.

It was obviously a devastating shock for Jay, his mum, and his sister, Hannah, who were all very involved in the life of our church. Gary and I had just been joking after the service the week before he passed. As I thought about this family, I reflected on what a devastating time it must be for them. With all the pain and shock that accompanies grief and loss, for Jay and Hannah there would be the realization that their dad would not be there to walk his daughter down the aisle, or enjoy the blessing of playing with his grandkids. In moments like this, we find it hard to understand what God is doing.

For a young guy like Jay, it was a critical time in terms of the glorious future that awaited him. In the face of personal loss, how would he respond? Some people lose their way in life's dark seasons and lose sight of their God-ordained future. Now a few years on, it's a joy to see how Jay and his sister are not allowing the shocking loss of their father, whom they dearly loved, to define their future. They have both continued to make wise choices that today has them flourishing in life, love, and leadership.

But this process can be so hard. When things come to an unexpected end, for so many people it can just build regret, disillusionment, and confusion. We feel guilty over mistakes we made when something comes to an end, and we realize that if we had just done things differently, maybe it wouldn't have ended this way. But when you follow Jesus, you have to trust that he leads you through those valleys, those places where the shadows gather and seem to blind your heart with darkness. He is the light and will lead you back to the green pastures and still waters. But it can feel very much like stumbling along in the dark, unsure of your next step and what you're bumping into along the way.

We have to remember God's promises in the truth of his Word. I love verses that encourage us to persevere. "For we have become partakers of Christ if we hold the beginning of our confidence steadfast to the end" (Heb. 3:14). When we begin the Christian life, it can be so exciting and new, so filled with a sense of wonder over God's grace and mercy. We start and the excitement carries us along until we hit a bump.

We're so confident, and then all of a sudden it seems all the forces of hell are lined up against us. We face a health crisis, an addiction, a job termination, a spouse's betrayal, a child's rebellion, a financial problem—sometimes all at once! Everything seems rigged to rob us of our dream, our hope, and our faith. But this is when we must remain steadfast, holding steady, keeping the confidence despite all the layers of hardship mounting around us. This is when the fabric of our faith is tested and feels as if it will give way, leaving us to fall into a pit of despair from which we can never return. Which is what the devil wants us to believe—but it's *not true*!

The truth is "He who has begun a good work in you will complete it until the day of Jesus Christ"! (Phil. 1:6).

Moments and Milestones

Once again, our Savior models this kind of trust in his Father's guidance even in his darkest moment, when completing his greatest sacrifice. He had been born in a manger, had lived as a man, revealed himself as the Messiah, taught and healed in public ministry, and endured the final suffering necessary to free us from our sins. With one last prophecy to fulfill, Christ recognized the end of his life as he had known it on earth.

> After this, Jesus, knowing that all things were now accomplished, that the Scripture might be fulfilled, said, "I thirst!" Now a vessel full of sour wine was sitting there; and they filled a sponge with sour wine, put it on hyssop, and put it to His mouth. So when Jesus had received the sour wine, He said, "It is finished!" And bowing His head, He gave up His spirit. (John 19:28–30)

Notice, however, that despite the pain he was in, the humiliation he suffered as an innocent man unjustly accused and unfairly treated, his executors could not break his spirit. Jesus willingly surrendered his spirit—he gave it up—after doing all he had set out to do in his public ministry. His death marked the end of an era, and his resurrection two days later would mark the beginning of another. Dying on the cross, Christ knew when he had reached the end point of his life as a mortal man.

But his life and ministry were far from over.

His body came back to life, to eat and drink and talk with his disciples, and revealed the power of God to defeat even death. He would spend forty more days on earth as a testament to his Father's power and glory before returning to his home in Heaven. But his ascension would also trigger another event that we've already explored: the gift of his Holy Spirit for his followers here on earth.

Christ died, was buried, and rose again, birthing the Church out of his painful death in the process. This explains the way he's described in the Book of Revelation as the Alpha and the Omega, the beginning and the end. We often see Jesus in the beginning of new endeavors and new relationships, but we rarely think about him being present in the end of them. And the more painful the ending or loss, the more difficult it can be to sense God's presence in our circumstances.

But he's there, loving us and urging us not to give up, helping us to mourn and grieve the past while remembering and entering into his glorious future for us. Everyone needs to remember that God goes before us, and even when we experience an unexpected stopping point or a slow, gradual one we see coming, either way he is present. He never leaves us.

The Bible is clear about the fact that our life has seasons, has a distinct rhythm, and so much of experiencing a big, spacious life is about living in harmony with the season we're in. Sometimes our lives have great, dramatic movements, and other times we feel caught in a rut with nothing much changing. Wherever we are, though, God is with us. In the transitions of life, we don't have to stop just because we reach the end of an era.

Back to the Future

I don't know how this applies to you, but I'm confident that all of us are in the midst of change in our lives. We all have to face endings and new beginnings, leaving things behind in prior seasons and past chapters and starting fresh, taking steps into a glorious future that's just around the bend. Our momentum and pace in life is never constant and uninterrupted. It's never "blessing, blessing, double blessing, blessing, triple blessing, and then quadra blessing!" While we always have some blessings in our lives, they're often mixed in with trials and challenges. Sometimes it feels like "two steps forward, one step back."

The people in life who have the greatest momentum often see their momentum hit the biggest target right in the middle, causing an explosion that sends them reeling, wondering how they'll ever begin again. This is when their faith is tested, and they realize that so much of life is out of their control. We have to rely on the love of our Father and trust him, even when it doesn't make sense from our limited perspective. We have to remember that our ways are not his ways.

In order to keep moving forward into your glorious future, especially as you face the end of an era in your life, I encourage you to do three things. First, always believe the best for the future. If you view the future out of our regret, out of our past, out of our disappointment, out of our hurt, then you lose sight of God's goodness. Hard, terrible, brutal things happen in life. Whether you're in an urban jungle facing terrorism or an African jungle fighting disease, you are surrounded by suffering of some kind virtually every day. All you have to do is live long enough, and you realize that life can be painful.

But no matter what you're facing or what's going on around you, you must believe the best for the future, in Jesus' name. If you believe that God is who he says he is, then you have to know that somehow through it all, a glorious future awaits. A future that will surprise you and fulfill your deepest longings. A future that will reflect God's goodness and power, that will reflect his glory and grace.

God has given us his Word on this future: "For I know the thoughts that I think toward you...thoughts of peace and not of evil, to give you a future and a hope" (Jer. 29:11). I love the context of this verse, a message from God delivered by his prophet Jeremiah to the people of Israel, who were held in captivity in Babylon; their dream was to return home to Jerusalem. They felt as if they were at the end of their dream, that they would never be free to return home again.

But the Lord never abandoned them. There in a place that seemed a dead end, a land of destruction where the people of Israel were displaced as captives, God's Word came to them. They were told, "Thus say the LORD of hosts, the God of Israel, to all who were carried away captive, whom I have caused to be carried away from Jerusalem to Babylon: Build houses and dwell in them; plant gardens and eat their fruit. Take wives and beget sons and daughters; and take wives for your sons and give your daughters to husbands, so that they may bear sons and daughters—that you may be increased there, and not diminished" (Jer. 29:4–6).

Their way of life as they once knew it has come to an end, and the future looks bleak. They're starving for hope, afraid to believe that the future could be even better than what they once experienced. And then God tells them that he has a glorious future for them. You don't build houses and start families or plant gardens and make a life if you don't expect to put down roots and stick around. God told them that their story wasn't over; the last chapter had not been written. He instructed them, "Seek the peace of the city where I have caused you to be carried away captive, and pray to the Lord for it; for in its peace you will have peace" (Jer. 29:7).

Goodness and Mercy

Please think about the place where you currently find yourself. Maybe a dream has dwindled or a once-promising season has ended in disappointment. Maybe you've lost the person or possibility most precious to you. You feel like giving up, unable and unwilling to believe that the future could ever be joyful again. These are the times when we must seek God's peace.

When you're faced with an impossible situation, remember that you serve a God for whom all things are possible. Ask him to give you his peace and assurance, the kind that "passes all understanding," the kind that may not seem to make sense given the circumstances. When you feel as if you're being held captive by fear, pray for peace for where you are and what you're facing. Hold fast with the confidence that you began with when you became a partaker of the gospel, persevering all the way to the end, believing the best for the future. Choose to see the right here and right now as where God has placed you and will bless you—just like the Israelites. Your present, as well as your future, are not unknown to God.

In the midst of our end points, we can't always see it, but God's got this incredible way of making things work his way. My oldest son, Joel, never showed much interest in piano lessons. I would drive him to his piano teacher's home and pause long enough to ensure he actually went in. Joel always showed a passion for music, and the artist in him would often sketch drawings and ideas related to using music to help hurting people.

Then in his midteens, he and a number of his church friends began to play music together, write songs, and they pulled together a band they called Able. As it turned out, they were surprisingly very good. Each of these young men loved the Lord, but they played mainstream music and attracted a following. They ended up auditioning and entering a "battle of the bands" competition, which was screened nationally on channel V, an Australian music channel that is very popular with young people. Amazingly, week after week the viewing audience continued to vote for Able.

In the end, it came down to two bands. The ironic thing is that the other band included Matt Crocker, a close friend of the boys in Able. So Joel and his friends went on to win the competition, and they saw their dreams ignited by the promise of a significant recording contract, part of the prize for winning the competition. However, not long after all this had happened, dynamics within the band changed rather abruptly, and just as they skirted the edge of their dreams, it all came to a sudden, crushing halt. After so much hard work and torturous anticipation, as you can imagine, it was a bitter disappointment.

But here's the amazing thing: The story wasn't over. Looking back several years later, it's unbelievable how God has used the young guys in the band (Marty Sampson in the early days, plus Joel, Mikey Chislett, and Matt Crocker) as they combined their gifts and pursued their dreams through Hillsong UNITED. Today, they're writing music, recording albums, touring the world, and having films made about them. God had a bigger plan than making them rock stars—he wanted them to impact generations with passionate worship songs and sound. One dream ended, but it led to the birth of something bigger and more meaningful than we could've ever imagined.

The same is true for you. Just because something's over, it's not the end! When Jesus said it was finished, his sacrifice was over, but we know that he wasn't finished. And in your life right now, something may be over, but Jesus' work in your life is far from over. Believe the best for your future! Take God's promise in Psalm 23:6 to heart:

Surely goodness and mercy shall follow *you*.

Surely goodness and mercy shall follow you *all* the days of your life.

The end of an era is not the completion of your destiny.

CHAPTER TWENTY

All Things New

You make all things new
Yesterday and forever
Your love never changing
This hope never fading
Hallelujah

"All Things New," Hillsong Music, 2014

How do you start the last chapter of a book? When I stopped to think about the message I want to resonate in your heart as you flip the final page and close the cover on this read—regardless of whatever season you're currently facing—this profoundly simple verse just kept coming to mind: "We know that all things work together for good to those who love God, to those who are the called according to His purpose" (Rom. 8:28).

All things.

Together for *good.*

Oh, what a great God we serve!

All Means All

God's Word is crystal clear that our Father is committed to seeing us through all things, committed to empowering us to live,
love, and lead a life of purpose, passion, power, and peace. In
him, we can find meaning in our everyday moments, hope in
our hurt, joy in the small things, and new life—born again with
expectation of a glorious future.

Consider this for your own life right now: *all things* working
together for good.

If you look up the Greek for the phrase translated as "all
things" here, you discover it means just that—everything, each
and every one of them, all-inclusive. In the Old Testament, the
Hebrew word for "all things" is just as all-encompassing. No
matter how you look at it in the Bible—and it's in Scripture 353
times total—*all things* means all things. Not just the good things
but all things. Every single thing that occurs in our lives and in
our world, God can work together for good as we love him and
live according to his purpose. Really, all things?

I have a dog called Bali, who is a poodle—or, to be exact,
a cavoodle, part cavalier and part poodle. Named by my son
Ben after one of his favorite surf destinations, Bali is eight years
old, very smart, and at times rebellious. When we're staying at
Sydney's Bondi Beach, I get up and take him out to do what
little dogs have to do in the morning, and that's where one of
his stubborn quirks causes a problem. Bali won't go while on his
lead, so you have to let him off the leash for him to sniff around
and then do his business.

Well, at Bondi Beach, the council inspectors are known to
be ruthless when it comes to spotting off-leash pets and are

reputed to be quick to issue on-the-spot steep fines to their own-
ers. Inspectors walk around with scanners to scan the animals
who these days are required to be microchipped for registration
purposes. (Sounds a little like the Book of Revelation, doesn't it?)
So there we were on this bright, sunny morning, perfectly happy
with life and initially oblivious to the city council van parked
on the grass nearby.

Unfortunately, it wasn't until after I let Bali off his lead to do
his thing that I noticed the inspector's van was stationed in the
direction Bali was headed. Seeing that trouble was brewing, but
being as discreet as I could possibly be, I was calling "Bali! Bali!"
with ever-increasing urgency as he chose to completely ignore me.
Of course he found his spot: directly in front of the patrol van.
Not the way I wanted to start my day. Sure enough, the inspector
got out of his vehicle and, with a gruff and officious tone, gave
me a little lecture about dogs off their lead, but at least on that
occasion, Bali escaped being scanned.

Simply put, life has moments that we would not describe as
good, some simple inconveniences and others serious trials. But
in case there is any doubt, let me drive the point home for you.
In Romans, the Bible is talking about ALL THINGS. *All things*
means inconvenient things, difficult things, upsetting things,
hurtful things, confusing things, unexpected things, frightening
things, painful things, shameful things, sorrowful things, and
uncertain things.

God wastes nothing, and somehow, he weaves everything
together for his glorious future, as only he can. *All things* includes
connections and disconnections, things coming together and
things falling apart, your best day and your worst day, opportunities gained and opportunities lost, good seasons and tough seasons, problems and solutions, conflicts and resolutions, trials and

triumphs, relationships and acquaintances, sickness and health, poverty and wealth.

I love the way *The Message* puts it: "That's why we can be so sure that every detail in our lives of love for God is worked into something good" (Rom. 8:28). Not everything is good, and not only good things happen to us, but we serve a God for whom all things work together for good—for those who love him, for those who are called according to his purpose.

This is not to diminish the hard things. The things impossible to understand and probably undeserved. It's to encourage you that in *all things*…he still has a glorious future in mind. When you love God, live for Christ, and lead by his Spirit, you unleash a glorious future into the present of each and every day.

My Last-Ever Dessert

Do you believe in New Year's resolutions? I think many of us see a new year as a new opportunity to live with resolve and change what has been. As if the sun rising on a new calendar year somehow brings with it added ability to lose weight, increase your financial prowess, or simply change what may have been a less than ideal year into a prosperous, memorable one. That said, I believe any resolve is good resolve, whether it's made on January 1 or June 1. In fact, I start most months with fresh resolve. It was going to be sugar-free September, and then overcoming October, say-no November, and on it goes.

I may have lightheartedly declared around the dinner table that "this will be my last-ever dessert" a few times, but I live with the belief that while there's life, there's hope. If I don't have any resolve in my life, there's absolutely no chance that anything is going to change.

However, it is only when we live our lives according to the Word of God that we understand it's not our efforts, it's not our striving, it's not what we can do in our own strength that's actually going to change anything. It's believing that God can cause things to work together for good as we simply live our lives loving him, live our lives called according to his purpose—this is what transforms us.

Maybe I'm just a positive person by nature, but I expect good things each day of every year, not just January 1. I believe without a doubt that every single moment of every single day, for all 365 days, can reveal God's goodness—in my life and in yours.

It doesn't always *feel* good, but can you see his goodness operating in your life right now, today? What things did you bring into this year? What things, either good or bad, are in front of you right now? And do you believe God is working them all together for his purpose?

I mentioned to you how much I love David's Psalms. I love them for David's honesty and for expressing those dark nights of the soul when God seems far away and we can't see his goodness. But I also love that regardless of those moments, David manages to trust in the Lord and move forward, resting in his confidence that God would see him through, making a way and revealing a glorious future. David writes, "You crown the year with Your goodness, and Your paths drip with abundance" (Ps. 65:11).

How would you live differently today if you believed deep down that God had crowned your year with his goodness? What would you dare to accomplish for his kingdom if you believed the path he has set you on drips with abundance?

He has...and he will. The God we serve has purpose and

plans for your life that are good. His thoughts about you are good; his will for you is good. All things are made new in his presence...your glorious future was planned before the foundations of the earth.

All Things New

Life is like art, in that you start with a blank piece of paper, a blank canvas, and you get to paint the picture. Maybe sometimes the picture gets a little smudged, or you have to incorporate a spill. But in the hands of the ultimate Artist and Creator, even these can become integral facets of the beauty of our lives. In his hands, all things—*all things*—are made new. "Therefore, if anyone is in Christ, he is a new creation; old things have passed away; behold, all things have become new" (2 Cor. 5:17).

God has given us our own will and our gifts and talents that we can live according to his calling and purpose. He's given us the opportunity to live a wide-open, spacious life, filled with opportunity to do the things we love and enjoy it with the people we love.

And even when we travel down the difficult path, don't underestimate his ability to make anything new. Maybe your heart's broken, it's crushed, but he can make it whole again. You might be dealing with a marriage falling apart or a family that seems to be unraveling in different directions. God can make them new again. He can take what seems impossible and transform it from the inside out.

No matter what things are going on in your life, if you just keep loving God and living your life called—living according to God's purpose—then ultimately he will orchestrate all things according to his will. If he has purposed it, he will accomplish it in Jesus' name. And the best news is that he is already at work in your life, shaping and shining, redeeming and revealing all his good plans for your future. Your Father is in control and makes all things new. There's nothing he can't fix. It's never too late.

When you walk through the narrow gate and allow God to make all things new in your life, you will experience the fullness of his glorious future being realized. He's given each of us a brand-new start in Jesus, and with his Spirit living inside you, you can finally start living the wide-open, abundant life you were meant to enjoy. The expansive, joyous excitement you feel on the inside of your life will spill over, and you'll see new victory and new vitality in your words, actions, and habits.

God can cause you to find abundance in all things, but it's got to start here. And if you're believing for all things to work together for good, then you will crave a steady diet of God's Word, drawn to the truth of his promises again and again. It's time to turn the page, allow God to orchestrate miracles out of mistakes, and transform you into his masterpiece. It's time to write a new chapter and believe the best stories are still untold, the best lines are still unwritten, and the best conclusion is the promise of eternity. He makes all things new.

All for the Glory

Last, but certainly not least, whether living in the wide-open, spacious places or traveling down the difficult path, living, loving, and leading like Jesus isn't all about us. It's about glorifying the Father. No matter what he was doing, Christ always reflected back to his Father's power, honor, goodness, grace, and holiness.

Recruiting fishermen to be his followers, he glorified God. Healing a blind man, he glorified God. Teaching in the synagogue, he glorified God. In life and in death, he glorified God in all things and in turn revealed the way God uses all things to bring about his good purpose.

We are told to do the same, revealing the light that is in us by how we conduct our lives. "If anyone ministers, let him do it as with the ability which God supplies, that in all things God may be glorified through Jesus Christ, to whom belong the glory and the dominion forever and ever" (1 Pet. 4:11). When things are going well, let's not forget to give God the glory, and when things are going terribly, let's not forget to give God the glory—because it's amazing how God will find glory in the worst circumstances if we trust him and put him first.

It has been sixteen years since that fateful day when my friend and colleague, George Aghajanian, concluded our weekly meeting with the terrible news and those crushing words, "It's not about you, it's about your father." That sentence was destined to bring my earthly father's past actions and their consequences crashing into my life, my leadership, and my world in a shocking, unwanted, and devastating manner. And now, after forty or more years, the skeleton of my father's sins has rattled yet again in the form of a public inquiry where my motives and those of others involved have been openly questioned, and my integrity has been assailed.

I believe with all my heart that I handled an impossible situation with transparency and honesty. In hindsight, could you do some things differently? Always. And yet I certainly did my best at the time with what I knew. Can such a tragic situation ultimately work for good? Is it possible that anything of worth can come from a circumstance where lives were shattered and deep pain was experienced? I cannot speak for the real victims of my father's actions, but I have seen firsthand the fallout among his children and his grandchildren. It has felt impossible at times to see how God can do something good with our worst days, or how God could ever be glorified in this—and yet I can already see glimpses of light at the end of a very dark tunnel. A tunnel that seems to go on and on into the deep face of an uncertain future.

The overwhelming support of so many wonderful people is certainly worth glorifying God for. The unwavering love and loyalty of our team is worth glorifying God for. The deep work that God has done and is doing in my soul is worth glorifying God for. If I am being honest, though I am somewhat disillusioned with the process, if justice and truth do finally prevail for innocent victims, and the future of safety for children can be secured through better policies and procedures—these outcomes are worth glorifying God for.

Paul says he knows how to be abased and how to abound, and either way he's learned to be content (see Phil. 4:12). It's amazing how God can reveal his glory when we remain faithful both in our reliance on him and our willingness to praise him regardless of our circumstances.

Often we see athletes in an interview after winning a big game say, "I just want to thank God and give him all the glory!" Or at the Oscars, we'll see an actor say, "I give God all the glory for this award! I never could have done it otherwise." Some people tend to roll their eyes and dismiss these professions of faith, but I believe we should take them as an indication of humility. The speaker is at least trying to take the focus off their own ability and talents and indicate that there's more to their big win. I'd rather see someone giving God the glory than taking all that glory for themselves, because if we commit our lives to glorifying God in all things, then I believe in all things we can see God bringing something good.

I know from experience that God can take anything and everything and use it in surprisingly glorious ways. Just look at my life. Even though we may not be able to see it, even though circumstances may seem unfair, even though it's not what we expected or it's not convenient, no matter what happens, we can learn to spot God's glory if we're committed to loving, living, and leading for him.

Remember, this may not look like circumstances changing, but to God, there is an eternal picture. Glorifying God is not about diminishing what has happened or is happening in your life, but about the promise that God will bring about new life. Our God is always at work restoring, and that work begins now. In fact, he is *at work*. Moving mountains, picking people up from the valleys, out of gutters, rescuing and redeeming, restoring and bringing hope. Having a faith perspective on life, love, and leadership isn't about playing down the difficulties of life—it's about being certain that God is bringing new life, both in the now and not yet of his kingdom.

Chapter upon chapter of this book, Hillsong Church—along with my own life—has seen each and every one of these seasons. Seasons of pioneering, seasons of consistency. Seasons of momentum and growth, and seasons of challenge and difficulty. We have experienced the peaks of the mountaintops and the steep walls of the valley. We've found our grace zone, and floundered in our humanity. But whether in seasons of stepping out of the boat or walking on water; whether in pioneering days or days of established comfort, we have allowed our continued prayer to be this:

> *Spirit lead me where my trust is without borders. Let me walk upon the waters, wherever you would call me. Take me deeper than my feet could ever wander, and my faith will be made stronger, in the presence of my Saviour.*
>
> *"Oceans," Hillsong Music, 2013*

So, whether you are searching for your calling or wholeheartedly pursuing your life's purpose, whether you find yourself wrapped up in the loving arms of our Heavenly Father or on your knees in desperation—be reminded again that he is the all-knowing, all-powerful, ever-gracious God of yesterday, today, and forever. He is trustworthy and he is faithful in all things.

Stay on this path, my friend. Follow Jesus, and God will crown you with his goodness. You have an amazing inheritance in Jesus' name, a mountain to summit and a path to pioneer. You have a faith lane that is all your own, a grace zone that is waiting for you to occupy. The difficult path and shame of your past is no match for his name, for his healing power, and for his holy calling. Your unique gifts are tailored perfectly to outwork his purpose in this generation and your wide-open, spacious, God-ordained life is waiting for you to jump right in! Live, love, and lead like Jesus and your life on earth and in Heaven will reflect the ongoing glory of God—in all things!

There is no doubt—your best is yet to come!

Hillsong Music Credits

"Desert Song"
Words and Music by Brooke Ligertwood
© 2008 Sony/ATV Music Publishing Australia (Aust. & NZ only), Hillsong Music Publishing (Rest of world)

"From the Inside Out"
Words and Music by Joel Houston
© 2005 Hillsong Music Publishing (APRA)

"This I Believe (The Creed)"
Words and Music by Matt Crocker & Ben Fielding
© 2014 Hillsong Music Publishing (APRA)

"With Everything"
Words and Music by Joel Houston
© 2008 Hillsong Music Publishing (APRA)

"No Other Name"
Words and Music by Joel Houston & Jonas Myrin
© 2014 Hillsong Music Publishing (APRA)

"Anchor"
Words and Music by Ben Fielding & Dean Ussher
© 2012 Hillsong Music Publishing (APRA)

"All I Need Is You"
Words and Music by Marty Sampson
© 2004 Hillsong Music Publishing (APRA)

"None But Jesus"
Words and Music by Brooke Ligertwood

© 2005 Sony/ATV Music Publishing Australia (Aust. & NZ only), Hillsong Music Publishing (Rest of world)

"Hosanna"
Words and Music by Brooke Ligertwood
© 2006 Sony/ATV Music Publishing Australia (Aust. & NZ Only), Hillsong Music Publishing (APRA) (Rest of world)

"All Things New"
Words and Music by Ben Fielding & Dean Ussher
© 2014 Hillsong Music Publishing (APRA)

"Saviour King"
Words and Music by Mia Fieldes & Marty Sampson
© 2006 Hillsong Music Publishing (APRA)

"I Give You My Heart"
Words and Music by Reuben Morgan
© 1995 Hillsong Music Publishing

"Glorious Ruins"
Words and Music by Matt Crocker & Joel Houston
© 2012 Hillsong Music Publishing (APRA)

"All Things New"
Words and Music by Ben Fielding & Dean Ussher
© 2014 Hillsong Music Publishing (APRA)

LET'S TALK LEADERSHIP

Stay tuned for more leadership resources from Pastor Brian Houston, INCLUDING "Let's Talk Leadership" and "Let's Talk Church"—a series designed to empower leaders from all walks of life and levels of influence.

For over 40 years, Pastor Brian Houston has endeavored to preach to people's "Monday's" and not just their Sundays. Meaning, his life and leadership is all about empowering people to fulfill their unique purpose and calling—taking the principles that they learn in church and enabling them to outwork these practical lessons in their home, workplace, and relationships.

Many have described him as leading the charge in generational leadership, creating a diverse and accessible intersection of church and culture. He is a sought after teacher and speaker and is regarded as one of the foremost voices on leadership and the local church.

For more information and to stay up to date with
Brian Houston, Hillsong Church, and Let's Talk Leadership,
visit **brianandbobbie.com** or connect through
social media below.

Follow Brian on Twitter: **@BrianCHouston**

Follow Brian on Instagram: **@BrianCHouston**

Like Brian & Bobbie on Facebook:
facebook.com/BrianAndBobbie

PODCASTS

Each and every day, thousands of people are accessing FREE audio podcasts from Pastor Brian Houston. These messages are created to bring hope and encouragement, to inspire generations of believers with practical and biblical teaching. Your work life, home life, and relationships matter to God—and they matter to us. Join thousands of others to receive free teaching that will unlock and unleash you to your greatest potential.

To access and subscribe to these life-giving messages, search for "Brian Houston" in the iTunes Store or Podcast App.

HILLSONG TV
WITH BRIAN HOUSTON

Each week, millions of people from 160 countries around the world tune into Hillsong Television with Brian Houston—a half-hour program straight from the platform of Hillsong Church. We receive letters every day from people whose lives have changed through the Word of God broadcast through their television screens—from the most remote villages to prison cells and living rooms, the gospel message of Jesus Christ is transforming lives. Join Pastor Brian Houston and Hillsong Church by watching youtube.com/hillsongchurchtv or visiting hillsongtv.com to see which channel Hillsong Television is broadcast on in your local area.

Bobbie Houston, as co-founder with her husband, Brian, of the Hillsong Church, shares her defining conviction about the feminine heart and God's intent for womanhood.

THE SISTERHOOD frames a 20-year journey—a portrait story that began with a whisper that has now grown into a global movement of everyday women across every continent of the earth. It is a modern-day "for such a time as this"—birthed from a mandate to place value upon womanhood and inspire women to be the change in their local community and setting. It's a story that embraces and captivates women of all age, status, background, and culture. It has redefined a new wineskin within the Church when it comes to the potential and ministry capacity within women.

Based in biblical truth, drawing from her own experience and with testimonies from around the world, Bobbie models the kind of tough-and-tender transparency that women find contagious. She reminds both men and women of what it means to be created in the divine image of God and what it means to complement and partner strategically in a gospel message that carries no bias or prejudice. With grace, candor, humor, and strength, Bobbie deeply encourages the sisterhood of women on the earth today to become pioneers of a new model of femininity—one forged by faith, nurtured by compassion, and sustained by love.

Bobbie founded the Colour Sisterhood in 1997, which finds expression in the Colour conference (hosted annually in Sydney, South Africa, London, Ukraine, and the USA). The foundation encourages and facilitates many humanitarian projects and initiatives.

MY MISSION

It was in 1993 when I sat down to write out a vision—a dream in my heart for a church that I longed to pastor. What I penned was indeed a visionary statement and a long way from the reality that we experienced then. By the grace of God, in many ways that vision, "The Church That I See," beautifully describes what God has built in our midst and perfectly encapsulates what many know today as Hillsong Church.

So it was on our 30th anniversary as a church in 2014 that I sat down once again to dream, pray, cast vision, and write a new and daring mission statement that would launch us—a now global church—into the next season of God's faithfulness and fruitfulness, and set the platform for generations to come...